"Thanks be to God for Tom Moore."

—LYNN SWANN,
Pro Football Hall of Fame Wide Receiver

"His contributions offensively? . . . He is one of the brightest minds to have ever coached in the game."

—BRUCE ARIANS,
Two-Time Associated Press NFL Coach of the Year,
Super Bowl Champion Head Coach with the Tampa Bay
Buccaneers, and Author of *The Quarterback Whisperer*

"Every team should have a Tom Moore. He was that good. . . . Tom Moore outcoached everybody. . . . He took players that maybe the other coaches couldn't have made winners out of, and he made winners out of them."

—WAYNE FONTES,
Detroit Lions Head Coach (1988–1996),
NFL Coach of the Year (1991)

"I've told my wife and my son, 'If it wasn't for this guy, Tom Moore, right here, you would not be living the way you're living right now.'"

—JAKE REED,
Twelve-year NFL Wide Receiver,
Minnesota Vikings and New Orleans Saints

THE
PLAYERS'
COACH

THE
PLAYERS'
COACH

TOM MOORE

with RICK STROUD

Foreword by Tony Dungy

DIVERSION
BOOKS

Diversion Books
A division of Diversion Publishing Corp.
www.diversionbooks.com

Diversion Books and colophon are registered trademarks of
Diversion Publishing Corp.

For more information, email info@diversionbooks.com

Hardcover ISBN: 9781635769852
e-ISBN: 9781635769746

Design by Neuwirth & Associates, Inc.
Cover design by Jonathan Sainsbury

Printed in the United States of America
1 3 5 7 9 10 8 6 4 2

Diversion books are available at special discounts for bulk purchases
in the US by corporations, institutions, and other organizations.
For more information, please contact admin@diversionbooks.com.

To my wife, Willie; daughter, Terry; and son, Danny . . . for all the sacrifices they made so I could live a dream.

—Tom Moore

To my wife, Valerie, who made all the best edits to my life. The love and sacrifice of my three children—Wes, Natasha, and Alexandra—inspire me every day to be better.

—Rick Stroud

CONTENTS

FOREWORD

by Tony Dungy
Member of the Pro Football Hall of Fame, Class of 2016

I HAVE KNOWN Tom Moore for fifty-one years and over that period of time our roles changed several times. The first eight years, Tom was my coach. He taught me, nurtured me, developed me, and helped me grow as a player. Then for the next eight years we were coworkers—coaches on the same staff under Chuck Noll with the Pittsburgh Steelers. After that we were competitors for thirteen years, going up against each other and matching wits and schemes for various teams. Then, in 2002, I became the head coach of the Indianapolis Colts and Tom was my offensive coordinator for seven years. He was instrumental in helping Peyton Manning develop into the most prolific quarterback of our time and in helping the Colts take home the Lombardi Trophy in Super Bowl XLI in 2007.

After the 2008 season, I retired from coaching, but Tom kept going. So, for the last fifteen years I have been an analyst for NBC and covered Tom as he continued to coach and develop young men. Included in that time was a victory by the Tampa Bay Bucs in Super Bowl LV where Tom helped Tom Brady secure his seventh Super Bowl ring.

That's fifty-one years of evolving and changing roles, but fortunately for me our *relationship* never changed. And that's because Tom Moore is first and foremost a coach. I learned what that meant when I joined Coach Noll's staff as a young assistant in 1981. I asked Coach Noll what my job would be as a coach, and he said it consisted of one thing: "To help the people around you be better. Help your players, the other coaches around you, and the staff to be the best that they can be." I can truly tell you that is the essence of Tom Moore. He has spent his entire adult life helping people be the best that they could be.

I really believe that Tom Moore has had the best career of any assistant football coach ever. He has coached sixty-three years, which is unbelievable in itself, but it's not just his longevity that has been amazing. And it's not just the results. Sure there are the championships you can point to and the four Super Bowl rings he owns. There are the multiple MVP awards for the quarterbacks he's coached—from Terry Bradshaw to Peyton Manning to Tom Brady. There are the Hall of Fame inductions of his former players such as Lynn Swann, John Stallworth, Barry Sanders, Edgerrin James, and Marvin Harrison. But those don't even tell the whole story. Because Tom didn't just help his great players. He helped *everyone* be better.

In the early 1970s, Tom helped Eddie McAshan at Georgia Tech navigate the difficulties of being the first Black quarterback to start a game for a major university in the Southeast. In the late '70s he helped a young kid at Minnesota by the name of Tony Dungy navigate the journey from college quarterback to professional safety to NFL coach. And I promise you I wouldn't have been able to do that without Tom's guidance. And those stories aren't unique. Over the years, Tom has helped hundreds of players and coaches become the best that they could be.

Because NFL football is such a popular sport, we have become very familiar with the names of the great head coaches over the years—Vince Lombardi, George Halas, Chuck Noll, Bill Walsh, Joe Gibbs, Bill Belichick. We know those names, and if you're a football fan you've been able to read about them. But assistant coaches are less well known and haven't always gotten the credit they deserve. I am so excited that Rick Stroud took on this project and helped Tom tell his story. I believe that when you have finished reading *The Players' Coach* you will know the story of the greatest assistant football coach in NFL history.

It Ain't Pressure

IT WAS *MONDAY NIGHT FOOTBALL* against the defending Super Bowl champion Buccaneers in Tampa, 2003. The Colts trailed by three touchdowns with 3:47 remaining in the game. Everything that could go wrong had gone wrong.

Worse yet, it was Tony Dungy's forty-second birthday and his first return to Tampa Bay, where he had coached for six seasons and built a championship-caliber team but had been fired for not getting them over the hump. He never mentioned what the game meant to him, but he didn't have to. We all knew, and we wanted to win it for our head coach.

WHEN TONY DUNGY'S NAME was announced as we ran out of the tunnel that night, he was caught off guard when a loud ovation erupted. I'm sure he shed a few tears.

He knew it was going to be a tough place to win. That Bucs defense was damn good. He had built it. Warren Sapp, Derrick Brooks, John Lynch, and Ronde Barber had picked up where they'd left off in dismantling the Raiders with five interceptions to win Super Bowl XXXVII.

They had only given up one touchdown in their first three games and still held onto the fewest yards allowed in the league by the time Hank Williams started singing, "Are you ready for some foot-ball?"

John Madden, who was calling the game with Al Michaels, compared them to the Steel Curtain defense and the '85 Bears.

The Bucs had a 21–0 lead two minutes into the second quarter. Even when we did something right, something went wrong. Need an example? Our Colts cornerback Mike Doss intercepted Brad Johnson in the first quarter, fumbled on the return, and the loose ball was scooped up by Keenan McCardell, who ran it in for a touchdown. It was one of three TDs McCardell would score that night.

"We couldn't have played much worse," Dungy told Lisa Guerrero, ABC's sideline reporter. "We've got to stop doing dumb things we normally don't do."

When Barber added a pick six to make it 35–14 with under four minutes remaining, you could imagine television sets and lights being clicked off all over America.

Tony was worried about the Bucs pass rush. He knew the mayhem Sapp and Simeon Rice could create when they pinned their ears back and teed off. Pretty soon, the quarterback would be getting hit like a piñata.

After Barber's pick six, Tony walked up to me and asked, "Should we take Peyton Manning out of the game?"

I said, "I wouldn't do that."

The sellout crowd at Raymond James Stadium had diminished considerably by then. More than half of the fans had headed for the parking lots. They didn't know what I believed.

We had Peyton Manning. This thing wasn't over.

I understood why Tony was worried. But during my time in Indy, Manning had only missed one snap due to injury. The key to everything was protection. If No. 18 got hurt, you could collect the songbooks because church was over.

Being down 21 points is one thing. But it's much worse when you're facing head coach Jon Gruden and Monte Kiffin, one of the greatest defensive coordinators in NFL history. The Bucs had only given up 86 yards to our offense by halftime. That's not good if you're the one calling the plays.

But as Chuck Noll always told us when I began coaching with the Steelers, "It ain't pressure if you know what you're doing."

The Bucs were rolling, and they let us know it, too. Keyshawn Johnson was mic'd up for the game. The year before, Marvin Harrison had set an NFL record for the most catches in a single season with 143. Early in the game, when Marvin caught a short pass by the sideline, Keyshawn said, "That's how he gets his catches, huh? And he's the best receiver in the NFL? And that's how he gets his catches?"

As it turned out, Keyshawn didn't finish the game. He had some sort of leg injury, and with the outcome seemingly not in doubt, he went to the locker room early.

Down 21, we received the kickoff and Brad Pyatt returned the ball to the 17-yard line. We scored, and Tony's decision to keep Peyton in the game seemed to have paid off.

But without recovering the ensuing onside kick, this baby was over.

Then, we got it.

Fortunately for us, the Bucs had lost their starting left cornerback, Brian Kelly. Marvin Harrison was wearing out his inexperienced replacement, Tim Wansley.

"I don't care who's covering me," Harrison said. "Just get me the ball."

We scored, stopped them, and scored again to tie the game. The Bucs tried a 62-yard field goal with Martin Gramatica that was blocked, and the game went into overtime.

The Bucs won the toss and drove the ball to our 41-yard line, but our defense forced them to punt. We took over on our own 13 and Peyton completed five of nine passes to set up Mike Vanderjagt's game-winning field goal.

We were all exhausted when that game ended, and I think a bunch of fans must have turned around and headed back to their seats when we started making our comeback.

We didn't get out of the stadium until after 2:00 a.m. for the short ride to the airport. This was before text messaging. When Peyton Manning got home, the voicemails on his phone confirmed what he already knew.

"We got back pretty late because it was a Monday night game," Manning said. "I checked the recorder around four in the morning. I checked the voicemails, and they all were the same. 'Really sorry you guys lost. Keep your head up. You'll get 'em next week.' I wanted to say, 'My head's just fine. We won the game. When it's playoff time in a few months and ya'll ask me for tickets, I'm going to remember who went to bed and gave up on us.'"

That game was really a springboard for us as a team. From then on, no matter the score or the opponent, we always knew we had a chance to win with Manning.

. . .

THREE SEASONS LATER, that belief was tested in what would become our signature win during my time with the Colts.

I'd had Peyton Manning since he was a rookie. Nobody prepared harder. He asked a million questions, and he demanded answers to everything the defense was doing. Before long, he could finish the play call as soon as I started making it.

It would've been malpractice not to give Peyton the latitude to change plays. We would get to the line of scrimmage quickly, and our speed-to-formation was helped by Marvin Harrison always lining up on the right side and Reggie Wayne on the left. We liked to go no-huddle because that would give Peyton more time to identify the defense.

I would give him concepts of plays that he knew would work against certain defenses. Peyton would make sure we got in the right play against the defense we were facing.

It all began in Week 14 of the 2000 season when we trailed the Jets 14–0. "Peyton!" I screamed. "We're going to run the no-huddle the rest of the game."

He nodded.

We lost the game, but on the plane ride home, Peyton asked, "Why are we waiting to get down fourteen points?" That's when "Lightning" was born. That's what we called our no-huddle attack.

But in this game against the Patriots, the AFC Championship Game, it was Tom Brady who was thundering away.

We fell behind 21–3. But nobody even blinked because we'd been there before.

"When we played a good Patriots team in the AFC Championship game and when Tom says, 'It's who plays the hardest the longest,' we've already done it." Dungy said, referring to the comeback over the Bucs.

Bill Belichick was very aggressive to start the game, going for it on fourth down near midfield where he normally might have punted. Much like the Tampa game, everything started to go wrong.

Running back Corey Dillon broke a big run and they scored when one of their offensive linemen recovered a fumble in the end zone. We kicked a field goal, but they marched right back down and scored a touchdown on the next possession.

Peyton threw an ill-advised pass, and it was intercepted and returned for a touchdown by Asante Samuel.

Manning had epic battles with the Patriots and Tom Brady. This was about to be one of them. And there were superstars and future Hall of Famers all over the field. But to this day, Belichick can't believe which players we used to beat them to move on to the Super Bowl.

Defensive lineman Dan Klecko caught a touchdown pass. Bryan Fletcher, our fourth receiver, had a huge 32-yard reception on a play he and Peyton had worked on all week. It was his only catch of the game. Joseph Addai scored the game-winner on a 3-yard run.

Before the AFC Championship Game, Belichick told me whoever won would go on to beat the Chicago Bears in the Super Bowl in Miami.

At the Pro Bowl that year, Belichick had a brief discussion with Peyton Manning about the AFC Championship Game.

"I don't mind getting beat by Marvin Harrison or Reggie Wayne," Belichick told Manning. "But how in the hell did you beat us with Klecko and Fletcher?"

What's crazy is that fourteen years later, I was on the Bucs' sideline when Tom Brady led our team to a 31–9 Super Bowl LV victory over the Chiefs and Patrick Mahomes.

.　　.　　.

I'VE ALWAYS BELIEVED that winning football is about the players, not the plays. And I've been fortunate to have coached so many outstanding players, legends of the game who are in the Pro Football Hall of Fame. I've also been blessed to be part of some of the biggest games, including winning four Super Bowls.

The credit all goes to the players, my fellow assistant coaches, and to the head coaches. I'm just the players' coach, a lifelong assistant, and that's okay. My job is to make the best players in the world even better.

1

Football Heaven

ON JUNE 29, 2023, I was given a place in Football Heaven. That's what the legendary John Madden called the Pro Football Hall of Fame. I was there to receive the Hall's Award of Excellence. And as I walked into the bust room on that hazy Canton, Ohio, morning—the room where the bronze likenesses of the greatest men in pro football reside in a sacred shrine—I felt blessed.

I'd coached in the National Football League for forty-five years, lived my dreams. I looked up toward the greater heaven, thinking about my guardian angels.

I have three and I wouldn't be here without them—my third-grade art teacher, Beverly Carpenter; my junior high basketball coach, Don Taft; and Forest Evashevski, my head football coach at Iowa.

I wasn't a star with the Hawkeyes. I knew my role. I was the best scout team quarterback in the Big 10, and I impersonated a lot of great quarterbacks in our conference. Back in those days, you didn't have specialists, so I was also a kicker. One time we were playing Ohio State in Columbus. It was a heated rivalry. Woody Hayes, the legendary Buckeyes coach, and Evy didn't see eye to eye. They were two big giants and there was only room for one.

It was late in the fourth quarter. A field goal wins the game. You miss it, you lose. So Evy grabbed me, stared into my eyes, and asked, "If I put you in to kick a field goal, can you make it?" I said, "Yeah, I can make it." He said, "Well, you better, or you better hope that Woody has a plane going back to Iowa City because you won't be riding on *our* plane." I don't think I took a breath until I kicked it and made it. I stayed on the field for the ensuing kickoff, and when I came back to the sideline, Evy said, "Nice job."

But I loved Evy, one of my angels. Did those angels bring me Terry Bradshaw, Peyton Manning, and Tom Brady to coach? No. I believe they brought *me* to them. That's how fortunate I felt to work with these great players.

I started my tour of the Hall of Fame bust room with the Class of '63—the first class enshrined. The faces of the league's most legendary figures—George Halas, Earl (Curley) Lambeau, Sammy Baugh, Tim Mara—stared back at me, probably wondering, "How the hell did they let you in here?"

I kept walking and when I got to Chuck Noll, I cried. Then, I thought of my father, who was one of the toughest guys I ever knew, a man who put down mile after of mile of railroad track. He once told me, "Little boys don't cry."

Yeah, but they didn't say anything about grown men.

In my football life, Chuck Noll was everything to me. He gave me my first chance to coach in the NFL. After I was hired, a Pittsburgh sportswriter named Vito Stellino asked me, "Hey,

Tom, they hired you as a college coach from the University of Minnesota and these guys have gone and won two Super Bowls. What do you bring to this program?" I said, "Hard work, Vito."

Well, after forty-five years in the NFL, I'm still working hard. I've won four Super Bowl rings—two with the Steelers, one with the Indianapolis Colts, and one with the Buccaneers.

After the 2009 season, I got the feeling that our Colts head coach, Jim Caldwell, may want to hire his own offensive coordinator. He promoted receivers coach Clyde Christensen to the role while I stayed in 2010 as the senior offensive assistant. The Colts lost in the AFC wild-card game to the New York Jets in what became my final year in Indianapolis. Both my knees were in bad shape.

I was only seventy-three, but Peyton Manning called my wife, Willie, at our Hilton Head home, and they secretly planned my career send-off. Or so they thought.

Willie sent Peyton a bunch of pictures from my time with the Pittsburgh Steelers and they made a cool collage. They had a highlight film made of some of the best moments of my career coaching in the NFL. They sent out invitations and gave me a big retirement party at Harry & Izzy's, one of the great steakhouses in Indianapolis.

They honored me at halftime at a game against Jacksonville that weekend. Before I walked to midfield, I put down my cane near the bench.

By then, I had received a call from Jets head coach Rex Ryan, who asked me to attend training camp, which I did for about six weeks.

About a month after the Colts honored me at halftime, Rex called again and asked me to serve as an offensive consultant for the last four games of the season. Of course, I accepted.

Peyton called me shortly after hearing the news. "You know, Tom, it doesn't seem fair," he said. "You got to kind of witness your own eulogy. I really feel like you ought to give me that video back."

Peyton knew better.

I'm a football lifer, the *assistant* my entire career in coaching and that's okay. I'm the players' coach. My job was to make the best even better. If you read my story, how it begins growing up in Rochester, Minnesota, without much, you'd know why I believe in guardian angels. I'm the most fortunate guy that God has ever created. At eighty-five, I'm still living my dream as a senior offensive consultant for the Tampa Bay Buccaneers.

Would I have liked to have been a head coach? Sure. But it didn't happen and that's okay. There can only be one general. If you can't be one, be the very best colonel.

I still get to work at 3:15 a.m. with pages of plays sketched in pencil on a legal pad. No iPads or computers for me. At least if we have a power outage, I'll still have a playbook. Why do I get up so early? Well, what am I supposed to do, lie there and stare at the ceiling? I'm eighty-five. I'm not sure how many days I've got left to live, but I know one thing: I'm not going to waste them sleeping. They're going to take me off the field boots-first.

For now, here in the Hall with Chuck and the busts of so many players I coached, I'm willing to pause and reminisce.

When Terry Robiskie, who coached about forty years in the NFL and was part of the inaugural class for the Award of Excellence, called me in Tampa to tell me I was going into the Hall, he very conveniently got me on a conference call with my daughter, Terry; my son, Danny; and my wife, Willie, so they could listen to him deliver the news.

Did I cry with my whole family on the line? Yes. When I saw Chuck's bust in the Hall of Fame, did I swell up again? Yes. Chuck gave me the chance to live my dream; my family supported me in pursuing it.

I've got a lot of stories about Chuck, one of the greatest all-time NFL coaches. One of the nicest men, too.

I remembered when Matt Millen, general manager of the Lions, interviewed me for their head coaching job in 2006. I didn't get it. But Millen called me up later and offered me a million dollars a year for four years. That's a lot of money. (The average assistant coach made about $300,000 that year.) And I didn't take it. The Lions hired Rod Marinelli, the defensive line coach in Tampa Bay, as their head coach. Detroit went 3-13 and then 0-16 the next two seasons. I knew unless I was going to be a head coach, I was right where I belonged in Indianapolis coaching on the same staff with Tony Dungy and working with Pro Football Hall of Fame players such as Peyton Manning, Marvin Harrison, and Edgerrin James. I eventually became his first offensive coordinator, designing plays and game plans for Bradshaw. Of course, he and so many of our Steelers players are in the Hall of Fame. So are two of the owners, Art Sr. and Dan Rooney. I can still smell Art Sr.'s cigar and hear that raspy voice of the Chief, as he was known to all.

The Steelers had already won two Super Bowls by the time I got to Pittsburgh in 1977. It was Mean Joe Greene and the Steel Curtain defense that got those Terrible Towels waving.

We changed all that. In 1978, they outlawed the bump-and-run because receivers couldn't get off the line of scrimmage once our cornerback Mel Blount got his hands on them.

That rule certainly helped our Hall of Fame receivers, Lynn Swann and John Stallworth. I saw Blount's bust right next to Bradshaw's as part of the Hall of Fame Class of '89.

5

Bradshaw got a bad rap. People said he wasn't smart just because he attended a southern school, Louisiana Tech, that wasn't a giant powerhouse, and his countryfied accent was thick as gumbo.

"When they're fussin' at me about the ol' 'I'm not very smart' thing, oh yeah, I'm not very smart, right? You believe that shit?" Terry would say. "Who called all those plays? Who threw those touchdowns? Who made those adjustments? I'd have to defend myself."

All I know is this: he won four Super Bowls, was the MVP of two of them, he's in the Hall, and he's the only Steeler with a star on the Hollywood Walk of Fame.

People say it's easy to win with Terry Bradshaw, Peyton Manning, and Tom Brady, guys whose busts will talk when they turn the lights out in the Hall of Fame, as John Madden surmised. What they don't say is you also won with Bubby Brister, Mark Malone, Scott Mitchell, and Carson Palmer, guys who would never be fitted for gold jackets. But let me tell you, they were tough guys and great quarterbacks. Mitchell was second only to Brett Favre in passing yardage in 1995, the year our Lions offense was tops in the league. Brister was part of Chuck Noll's final postseason run in 1989, beating the Oilers on the road in the wildcard. Malone had the unenviable job of following Bradshaw, but he was a first-round pick and led us to the playoffs in 1984. Carson Palmer in Arizona had his share of injuries. But he was the No. 1 overall pick of the Bengals and had flawless mechanics throwing the football. But none of them had the Steel Curtain defense in its prime or two Hall of Fame receivers and a running back slashing his way to Canton.

Down the line I went through the bust room with all those faces—familiar but frozen—marking the years of my life's journey. I felt so thankful to have my wife and two kids, their families, and many of our close friends with me.

Our Steelers teams alone from the '70s have fifteen busts, including Art Sr. and Dan Rooney, Chuck Noll, Tony Dungy, Bradshaw, Swann, and Stallworth, center Mike Webster, running back Franco Harris, Mel Blount, linebackers Jack Lambert and Jack Ham, defensive back Donnie Shell, defensive lineman Mean Joe Greene, and scout Bill Nunn.

Barry Sanders was part of the Class of 2004 and the centerpiece of our Lions' offense when I worked there for Wayne Fontes. Barry was a spectacular running back, and I don't remember him ever taking a direct hit.

I had a lot of great ones, including the Colts' Edgerrin James, who was enshrined with the Class of 2020. And the receivers. It didn't stop at Pittsburgh. I coached Cris Carter with the Vikings, who had the strongest hands I'd ever seen.

When Peyton Manning was inducted in 2021, Tom Brady chartered a private jet from Tampa to Canton so all of us former Colts coaches like Bruce Arians and Clyde Christensen could celebrate with him during an off-day at training camp. Also there was Bill Polian and Marvin Harrison, who had been inducted into the Hall of Fame and were waiting for Peyton. And we're all waiting for Reggie Wayne and Jeff Saturday to go into Canton, Ohio, one day.

But there was nobody in that hallowed Hall I've known longer than or am closer to than Tony Dungy. That stoic face carved from clay wasn't always that way. Believe it or not, when I recruited him to play quarterback at the University of Minnesota, I had to sit him down and tell him to control his emotions on the field.

He played for me, he coached with me on Chuck Noll's staff in Pittsburgh and on Denny Green's staff with the Vikings, and he was my boss as head coach for the Colts.

"It was so uncomfortable for me," Tony has said about the situation. "It was just total role reversal. But Tom was the ultimate assistant coach and that's the way Tom treated it. He was always making sure he didn't go above my head, even though I told him, 'You know what's right.' But that was hard for me. I'm thinking back to when I was seventeen years old and he's telling me everything, so now I'm supposed to be in charge and make decisions. It was just hard. But I felt so calm. I never had to worry about the offense."

I think it was sometimes unnatural for him not to call me Coach Moore, but like I said, I knew my place. I was the assistant and Tony was the head coach.

I have been an assistant coach my entire NFL career. And that's okay. For me, coaching in the NFL has been a privilege.

2

Peeling Back
My Steel Curtain

"WHAT Y'ALL DOIN' down here?"

It was 1961, and I had recently graduated from the University of Iowa—where I'd done one semester of engineering before deciding that, eventually, I wanted to go to law school. At the encouragement of one of my professors, a University of Florida alum, I'd applied to and been accepted into that school's law program. I'd gotten an apartment down there and showed up a week early to get the lay of the land.

When I told the barflies at the joint across the street from campus that I was from Minnesota, they looked at me with puzzled expressions and 'Ya'lled" me out. Same thing happened at a few other places. Then I went to Morrison's Cafeteria there in Gainesville. I went through and filled up my tray, and an elderly Black gentlemen said, "I'll take your tray to your table." I said, "No, I got it." He said, "You don't understand, sir. I have to take it."

I decided as a Yankee down there, I wasn't going to win any ties with the judge. So I left for law school back home in Iowa. I did one semester and knew the legal field wasn't my cup of tea. Just wasn't me.

No, I didn't belong in Gainesville in the early 1960s, and I didn't belong sitting on my ass in classrooms filled with future attorneys.

So, while throwing away my legalese textbooks and signing up for some other postgraduate classes, I talked with Forest Evashevski, "Evy," who had been my head football coach in my undergraduate days.

Just like he had during my recruiting trip years ago, he asked me a simple question: "What do you want to do?"

I told him I wanted to coach. As a Reserved Officers' Training Corp guy, my orders from the Army were to report at the end of November 1962 to begin basic training. So, I had some time, and Evy said, "Okay, you can coach the freshman team."

I had a great experience that summer because Eddie Robinson, the Grambling State head coach, was also going to summer school and working on his master's at Iowa. He ran the same Wing-T offense that Iowa ran. So, after class in the mornings, we spent the afternoons watching film of the Wing-T. Eddie was spectacular. He was a sharp man.

The Lord works in mysterious ways. Maybe it was meant that he should be at a historically Black school like Grambling State instead of a large football factory like LSU because all those players needed him.

After we played our last game, I drove from South Bend, Indiana, to Fort Benning, Georgia, and was there for eight weeks for basic training. We were the last class in 1962 and got sent to Korea. After that, they started sending guys to Vietnam.

We got off the plane in Korea and there was a big sign that said LOS ANGELES 7,825 MILES.

IT'S JUST OVER TEN MILES from Los Angeles to Pasadena, where the Rose Bowl sits. And all the way around the globe, I thought about how Iowa had been my ticket to that legendary stadium and game. Way back while living in Mt. Pleasant, Coach Evashevski spoke at a banquet my dad and I attended. In addition to being the head coach at Iowa, he had been Tommy Harmon's blocking back at Michigan. I was captivated by his speech. I looked up to him. I was in awe, frankly. I remember walking home with my dad saying, "I don't know if I will ever be big enough or good enough, but if I am, that's who I want to play for."

During my recruiting trips toward the end of high school, the best piece of advice I got was from Lenny Dawson. I visited Purdue, and the future Super Bowl champion Chiefs quarterback was my host. He showed me around, and at lunch I asked him, "What's the story on Purdue?" He said, "Let me give you some advice. I love Purdue. But go where you like the coaches and you're going to be happy and you're going to play. Don't worry about the education. You'll get the education because they got the same books in the library wherever you go."

After high school, a friend recommended me to Iowa, and they recruited me. I went down there for my visit. As I stepped into Evy's office, he asked me, "Tom, what do you want to do?" I said, "Coach, I want to go to the University of Iowa." He told me, "It's a done deal. You've got a scholarship and you're a Hawkeye."

I've had a lot of great moments in my life, but that was one of the greatest. I was able to tell my parents they didn't have to worry about sending me to college. I had a scholarship.

I thought I was a good quarterback, but freshmen couldn't play on the varsity back then. Our varsity quarterback at Iowa was Randy Duncan my sophomore year. He was an All-American, and Green Bay would select him as the first overall pick in the 1959 NFL Draft. Randy was good enough to keep me from being under center much, but I became the kicker because, in those days, there were no specialists. You played offense and defense and had to contribute on special teams. I got to play in the Rose Bowl as a backup, and that's okay. As a kid in the Midwest who loved football, I dreamed of being on a team that went to the Rose Bowl, and I fulfilled that dream.

As an undergrad at Iowa, I graduated in four years and—in all honesty—didn't feel like it was too taxing. To me, it was a job. I was always through by 11:30 a.m. and went to the library until I had to go to practice. I took fifteen credit hours a semester. When I got to the Pittsburgh Steelers later in life, Chuck Noll told me he took twenty-one. His thinking was, "If it was free, I'm going to go get as much education as I can."

I was in ROTC and then Advanced ROTC. My half-brother had been in the Battle of the Bulge in the Army. With my dad, it wasn't even discussed whether you were going to serve. It was a matter of which branch or service you were going into. He didn't give you many direct orders, but I got one that day. He said, "Your half-brother went. This country has been good to you. You're going to the service."

If I'm going, I thought to myself, I'm going in as an officer. With Iowa being a land grant school, ROTC was compulsory your first two years in those days. After that, I went advanced.

Funny story. Between your junior and senior year, you had to go to summer camp for six weeks. This is where the officers beat up on you and treat you like an enlisted man. You get four hours of sleep and they're constantly on your ass to see if they can break you, and they broke a few guys. If you had to wear a helmet, like in the daily drills, you also had to carry a fatigue hat. You put that inside your blouse or shirt. We were in formation one day and I had my helmet on but didn't have my fatigue hat tucked in very well. The captain walked by and said, "Cadet! Are you pregnant?"

I said, "No, sir, but I got fucked when I got into this outfit." He said, "Get down and give me fifty push-ups." He came by later in the day and pulled me off to the side and said, "That was pretty funny."

When our ROTC cadets came back from summer camp, we had a commander named Colonel Call who liked football. We had this big military ball. Colonel Call said, "You're in charge of selecting the honorary Cadet Colonel, the queen of the military ball." That was my project, so I did it. I asked her for a date to the military ball, too, because I knew who the queen was going to be. That's what you call inside information. This was in the spring of '61. Students were already starting to question our involvement in Vietnam.

The girl and I and the colonel and his wife were in this car going to the student union where the military ball was being held. There were all these students outside protesting. Colonel was a fiery guy, and he wanted to go after them. I wound up holding him back, saying, "No! No! No! Colonel, you can't do that."

．　．　．

I'D FIND OUT AFTER COLLEGE that something you *could do* in the military was coach football. In Korea, you got on the bus, and they took you to your duty station. I was the last sonofabitch on the bus. They dropped my ass off so far north, you could see the DMZ. Little fights were going on, but the conflict was over. We walked the DMZ and the North Koreans walked the DMZ, and we were on constant alert. I was in the Eighth Cavalry (which was also part of the First Cavalry Divsion). The Imjin River had a Freedom Bridge. Near Panmunjon, they had the Libby Bridge. I went up to see the colonel and he told us our mission. The bridges were loaded with explosives. In the forward areas, there were minefields all over. If the enemy came, once they got to the minefields, our mission was to blow the bridges up. If we could delay them sixteen minutes, then the jets from Osan would be there.

I said, "So our job is to blow the bridges up? So that means we're not getting out." He said, "We'll see."

You had to go to the officers' club three nights a week because they had some suicides. They wanted to make sure you weren't homesick. They were checking on us because we sat in our barracks a lot. About the third or fourth week, I was talking to the colonel. He said, "How's it going, Tom?" I said, "It's good." He said, "Are you enjoying it?" I said, "Yeah, I'm enjoying it. But really, I'm a football coach."

I told him I had played at Iowa. He said, "Our division sports officer is rotating back to the States. I know the general. I'll call him up."

I went to see General Clayman. To make a long story short, I became the division sports officer and head football coach of the First Cavalry Division. The Army had four teams in Korea. We also had two teams in Okinawa, and we had two teams in Japan. So all the teams played each other twice for entertainment for the troops.

My football team was 8–4 in the regular season and went to play the Air Force in the Sukiyaki Bowl in Okinawa.

From there, I was sent to Fort Benning, Georgia, where soldiers commissioned out of college went for three months for basic training. Our commanding general really wanted a good football team to compete against all the other bases for the service championship. We'd pull the orders of about two dozen players to stay on after their training.

At Fort Benning, we had a major who was the head coach (well, in title only) and I ran the offense. Another coach ran the defense. One of our players at Fort Benning was Pat Dye, who would become a legendary coach at Auburn. Pound for pound, he may have been the toughest player I ever coached. It was one-platoon football. Players went both ways, and he starred for us at guard and linebacker.

I think we ended up 11–1 and played Fort Eustis in what became the Citrus Bowl, but at the time was the Missile Bowl. We beat them. After that, I got out of the Army, and I wanted to coach professionally.

I CERTAINLY HAD the sports bug there during my military service, but I'd caught it back as a youngster in Iowa as the Second World War raged on. When the war started, we moved to Burlington, Iowa, and then to Mt. Pleasant, Iowa. My father got a job at the Iowa Ordnance Plant in Middletown, Iowa, where they made ammunition and bombs for the military. I remember the blackouts. I remember the rationing of coffee, gasoline, sugar, all those things. I remember VJ Day and there was such a celebration going. Car horns were blowing. People were going crazy, and it was traumatic for a kid. I was seven years old when the war ended.

Mrs. Carpenter, my elementary-school art teacher and the first of the three people in my life I consider my guardian angels, took care of me and guided me because my dad was working and my mother was working. Beverly Carpenter (more about her later) was very influential until I got to fifth grade. That's when I got involved in sports. This is where this whole thing took off with athletics.

We started playing football in fifth grade and the coach was Don Taft. He was my second guardian angel.

I got good grades, but I wasn't the smartest guy in the world. I probably wasn't the best-looking guy in the world, either. I sure didn't have money and I wasn't the best-dressed guy in the world. But I could compete in athletics. I was good at that level, so I saw sports as my path to have some success in life.

Coach Taft was a great person. We had fifth-, sixth-, seventh-, and eighth-grade teams. We won forty-eight games in a row in football. We won a lot of basketball games and we won a lot of track meets. I could compete, and that's the way I could get my recognition, in athletics. He was good to me, and I'll never forget the art teacher and the grade school coach because they made such an impression and helped me with their guidance and friendship.

DISCHARGED FROM THE ARMY in '65, I got an interview for a high school job in Grenell, Iowa. But it didn't feel right. I told my wife,

"I'm going to get a college job or go back to law school." Not that I was too good to coach teenagers or anything; I just wanted to coach in college. I talked to Jerry Burns, who was the head coach at Iowa at the time, and things weren't going great. He told me to come to Chicago for the national coaches' convention. He talked to his friend Henry (Hank) Bullough from Michigan State. John McVay had just gotten the head coaching job at Dayton and had been with Hank on the Spartans' staff. Henry talked to John and said, "Jerry Burns has got this guy who just got out of the Army, and he wants to coach." I interviewed with John, and he hired me to coach the freshman team.

I want to say a couple things about John McVay, who should be in the Pro Football Hall of Fame for what he did in his career as the head coach of the New York Giants and especially for the team he built for Eddie DeBartolo, Bill Walsh, and the San Francisco 49ers.

He simply was one of nicest men I ever worked for and incredibly smart. He was very deliberate and a great listener. Case in point: He invited me and the other three coaches he'd hired down to Dayton the next weekend. He had us bring our wives. Then he did something I thought was great.

We had the jobs if we wanted them. But he insisted on talking to our wives, and he explained to them what college coaching was like. He gave them the timeframes and schedules that we were going to follow, everything from the offseason recruiting periods to the summer vacation time. Everything was enumerated because he didn't want there to be any surprises.

He did that on Saturday and he told us to meet with him again Sunday and let him know if we still wanted the job. Obviously, I took it and so did George Perles, Jerry Hanlon, and Joe Eaglowski. I was now in college coaching.

John had assembled his staff at Dayton. Jerry Hanlon, for example, would go on to coach the offensive line for Bo Schembechler at Miami of Ohio.

I was going to coach the freshman team and also coach quarterbacks. John said, "I can't give you much money." I've never been in this profession to see how much money I could make. They gave me $6,000. They got my wife a job in the library making $1,500. George, Jerry, and Joe got $8,000, and we had a ball. After the first year, Jerry left and that's when they hired Wayne Fontes, who was a great high school coach in Bay City, Michigan.

Of course, many years later, Wayne would hire me as offensive coordinator with the Detroit Lions after he got the head coaching job there.

AT DAYTON, the football program hadn't been very good, and our first year there didn't go well. The varsity team won 1 game, lost 8, and tied 1. There was some real work to be done. But I knew about work.

As a kid, in addition to sports, I had to make money. The first job where I made money was tying wires on a hay baler. I was ten years old. I got a penny a bale, and on a good day, you could do one thousand bales of hay. That's $10 a day, pretty good money. You had to wait until the sun was high enough for the dew to dry off the hay, which was about nine thirty or ten in the morning. You worked until the dew came back, which was about 6:00 p.m.

I graduated from that job in about two years and then detasseled corn for Cargill Corn Company. You contracted four acres, and when the tassels came out, you'd detassel six rows and leave two rows of tassel and then the tassels would pollinate the six rows and that's how you got your hybrid seed corn. Usually, you had to work every day for about ten days to get that done. You got $60, or about $6 per day. That was good money back then in the early '50s.

A lesson I learned from this and from my dad was that once you started something, once you committed to it, you didn't quit. After detasseling corn for a couple days, I told my dad, "I don't like this." He said, "It don't make any difference if you like it or not, you signed a contract, so you do it. Once you're committed, there is no quit." That's the way I was brought up.

I also learned at a very early age that one of the keys to work ethic and respect for others is to be on time. My dad only got one week of vacation from the railroad. Because he got free train passes, we'd go to Chicago and watch the Chicago Cubs play. I went to my first game in 1946. It was the Cubs against the Boston Braves. That was kind of a ritual for five or six years. One night, I was supposed to be home at 5:00 p.m. and I didn't get home until six thirty. My dad said, "You're late, aren't you?" I told him, yes, I was late. I was also young and kind of stupid. He said, "You're not going on vacation (which was a weekend) this year. I've talked to neighbors and you're going to stay with them. Your brother, mother, and I will go to Chicago and you're not going this year because I told you to be home at five and you're coming in at six thirty. If you're two minutes late, at least you're trying to get there. When you're ninety minutes late, you're telling me you don't care." We got that squared away pretty quick. I haven't been late to anything for the rest of my life, trust me.

*　*　*

THE DAYTON FRESHMAN team I coached went 5–1. We played Xavier and Miami (Ohio), Cincinnati and Kent State and some similar schools. Then, the next year, they hired another freshman coach, and I moved to varsity full-time. That year, Dayton's varsity squad went 8–2.

We'd have some great battles in practice. It was always between me and Wayne Fontes, who ran the defense. One thing about coaching: you can guarantee that 100 percent of the time, 50 percent of the coaches are pissed off and 50 percent are happy.

"I was amazed at how important little details were to Tom," Fontes says. "He was a stickler for making sure everything was ready to go at any time. If something wasn't going right, he knew exactly how to fix it. He was prepared. At Dayton, the players rallied around him."

ONE THING I COULDN'T FIX while I was coaching at Dayton was my father's ailing health. I think about my parents often. They were such good people, and I didn't appreciate them like I should have because I was young. In 1966, I came home for Christmas after my father had suffered a minor stroke. He had gotten all his faculties back and the last thing he ever told me before I left to return to the Flyers was, "Tom, I know everything hasn't been perfect. But let me tell you this. I tried. I tried as hard as I could. And I love you and this will probably be the last time we ever see each other. I just want one promise from you. Promise me you'll take care of your mother." I said my brother and I would.

In April of 1967, he was at home and woke up one morning. My mother was in the kitchen, and he called her into the bedroom. He looked at her and said, "I think it's over." Then he lay down and died. Neither of my parents graduated from high school and my mother had done well to work as a registered nurse and self-trained anesthesiologist. I think of all my father went through and had to overcome. He worked on the railroad until he was seventy-two just to take a job taking care of a racehorse. I think of my mother getting up at three in the morning to bake pies. Well, then I hear people complain. It really turns me off. I would never complain about anything because I know how much better I've had it in life than my parents.

I THREW EVERYTHING I HAD into football at Dayton, and I was surrounded by guys that did the same. We competed like hell in practice, especially during end-of-game situations. John would say, "Last drive, so many seconds on the clock. We need to score a touchdown to win."

Well, Wayne and his staff weren't opposed to doing anything they could to win. Wayne tells this story about one of our practices.

"Their offense is moving down, moving down, and all the sudden they get to the 3-yard line and John McVay says, 'Okay, you get one last play,'" Fontes said. "George stuck his head in the huddle and said, 'Look, we can't let these guys in.' It became personal.

"It was Perles and myself against McVay and Tom Moore. George calls the defense, and I said, 'If they come out, I'm going to go stand where I think the ball will go.' They broke the huddle and they put one receiver wide, and I know they're going to throw a slant. So I walk off and George waves at me and I go stand right where the slant is supposed to go. Tom Moore looked up and saw me standing there, so they called an audible and ran a trap. They snapped the ball, and the guy gets trapped and the hole opens and they're going to score. That's when George Perles stood up and hit the running back dead in the hole and the guy went down. The defense was screaming and yelling and picked up George Perles and carried him off the field."

John McVay was standing behind the offense watching the scrimmage. I could tell he was amused by it.

Afterward, I was pissed, but I thought it was kind of funny. I went up to John and said, "It's hard to beat thirteen guys!"

Little did I know, the way George stood up that running back? He would stand on the table the same way for me with Chuck Noll. George was responsible for my being hired by the Pittsburgh Steelers and for my career in the NFL.

3

Help Us Become Great

THE STEELERS TRAILED the Oakland Raiders 7–6 after Kenny Stabler scrambled into the end zone from 30 yards away. There were 73 seconds remaining in the divisional playoff game on December 23, 1972.

Art Rooney Sr. had just begun to make his way down from the owner's box at Three Rivers Stadium to console his players and coaches in the locker room, when—after three incompletions by Terry Bradshaw—the Steelers faced fourth-and-10 from the Pittsburgh 40 with 22 seconds left in the game.

Running back Franco Harris's job on the play was to stay in and block, but when Bradshaw rolled to his right, he instinctively took off downfield.

Bradshaw stopped and attempted a pass toward the middle of the field to Frenchy Fuqua, who was breaking open. But Raiders safety Jack Tatum, one of the fiercest hitters in the game, zeroed in on the back of Fuqua and arrived with the football.

After an enormous collision the football caromed about five yards into the outstretched hands of Harris, who had played running back at Penn State, where Joe Paterno always told his players to "Run to the ball! Run to the ball!"

That's what Franco did, and his historic play resulted in the game-winning touchdown and arguments that have lasted until this day.

When Chief got downstairs, he asked, "What happened?" Mr. Rooney didn't get to see the Immaculate Reception. A stadium guard ran toward him and said, "You won it!" Rooney replied, "What?!"

Today, the statue of the Immaculate Reception greets you just before reaching the escalators in the lobby of Pittsburgh International Airport. A life-sized sculpture of Franco Harris in his black and gold Steelers uniform is bent at the waist and plucking the football just above his shins.

It's one of the most controversial and iconic plays in NFL history.

UNLIKE HARRIS'S RECEPTION, I wouldn't call my childhood *immaculate*. But when I look back, I realize it was a lot better than most, and I owe my parents my deepest gratitude. If I had one wish in life, it would be that I could see my mother and father again just for an hour. As a kid, I was aggressive and outgoing and wanted to make things happen. They really didn't understand me, and I didn't understand them. I didn't understand what my father, Howard, was going through. He was such a proud person and I think he was embarrassed that he couldn't do more. I didn't make it easy for him, which I regret. I was wrong. I wish I could tell them both I understand now, and I'd apologize. I wish I could make it up to them because they were both great and wonderful people.

My father was fifty-five years old when I was born. My mother, Emma, was his third wife. She was forty-three. His first wife died in the 1918 flu epidemic. He remarried, but his second wife would take his two kids to the movie theater and just leave them there while he was working. My father found out about it and divorced her.

It wasn't the life he thought he was going to live. My dad was from an Irish family in Iowa. They farmed, and at a very young age, he owned three grain elevators. But two days before the stock market crash when they closed all the banks, he had deposited $25,000 in the bank and lost it all. It ruined him, not just financially, but I think spiritually, as well.

I mean, think about it. He's got a wife who died and left him to care for their two very young children: my half-brother, Bill, who was a juvenile diabetic, and my half-sister, Marjorie, who contracted polio in 1948 during the epidemic of that crippling disease.

He's lost all his money. I mean he had no money. None. Zero. He's sort of on the bum. He's taking care of my half-brother and getting help with my half-sister. He told us stories about the Great Depression that are mind-boggling.

I didn't realize the mental anguish he felt. Every Christmas was ruined because he was drunk. He was a binge drinker. He was embarrassed. We never had many Christmas presents. I stole a Christmas tree so we could have one. I wasn't as nice as I should've been, but my father told me, "You've got your health and your freedom, so get a life."

* * *

AFTER MY FATHER DIED, I spent two more years at Dayton—and I often thought about how I could pay things forward, as they say, and make him proud. I had chosen my profession, and I was determined to get to the highest level and to excel. I'd taken a job coaching at the University of Minnesota, and in 1972 I was calling plays for my quarterback, Tony Dungy. Tony's freshman year, I took a chance by joining the New York Stars of the newly formed World League. That was a classic example of what Chuck Noll told me one time, that "sometimes the grass is greener around the septic tank." Babe Parilli, who had worked for Chuck Noll and the Steelers, was the head coach. Because of that, I got to learn the Steelers offense. When I interviewed with Chuck Noll a few years later, I had to let him know I wasn't trying to pull one over on him. I'd just had a year coaching in his offense.

The Stars moved in 1974 and they became the Charlotte Hornets by the end of their first year. However, my family had to move four times that year.

One time, we were playing a game against the Houston Texans of the WFL, and they had John Matuszak, who also was under contract with the Oilers at that time. He played a total of seven plays before a restraining order was served to him mid-game, banning him from playing for two teams at the same time.

When we moved to Charlotte in the middle of the '74 season, we didn't get paid anymore. I was going to last until the first of March, or I was going to be a bartender or something. By February 27, I had three job offers. I decided to go back to Minnesota because Tony was still there, and I was grateful Cal Stoll took me back.

I was dead broke. George Perles, whom I had coached with at Dayton, lent me $5,000. If I hadn't stayed in football, I'm not exactly sure what I would've done. While I was at Iowa, I earned my teaching certificate, and while coaching at Dayton, I got my master's degree in guidance counseling, so I probably would've gotten a job in some high school as a teacher or guidance coun- selor or coached physical education and been a bartender at night. It was a scary situation, but my wife and children said, "Don't worry about it, because we're with you." If my mom can get up at three in the morning and make pies for a restaurant every day so her kids can eat, and my dad can sleep in a stall to calm a horse down, I thought my potential problems were very minimal.

I was able to pay the loan back to Perles when I went to the Steelers and we won a Super Bowl and I had extra earnings from that game. The loan was all interest-free. You know how you have real friends and you have pretenders? Well, George was a real friend.

Anyway, after the Steelers beat Oakland with the Immaculate Reception, they were slated to play Miami. I was all fired up for Perles, who was now an assistant head coach of the Steelers. So I told my wife, "Let's fly to Pittsburgh and watch the champi- onship game." We flew in, I called George, and I went to the field and met head coach Chuck Noll at Saturday's practice. He knew I had coached with George at Dayton, which was a good place to start a conversation because Chuck had gone to school and played football there. He loved Dayton.

The next time I met Chuck Noll, I was interviewing for a job on the Steelers staff coaching receivers.

I had two advantages by the time there was an opening on the Steelers staff. Since Babe Parilli ran the Steelers offense with the Stars, I already knew it.

But I owe Perles for helping me get the job in Pittsburgh. George really stood up for me.

I was finally in Pittsburgh, going through a very long and thorough interview with Chuck Noll. It probably lasted eight hours. It was a great interview. He said, "I'm your receiver. You just drafted me. Teach me." That was his thing. Some people were presenters, and then there were the *teachers*.

"Okay, you told me to run a hook route, but how do you want me to run it? What if it's man off? Or inside man press? Zone or man rotation? How do you want me to run these routes?"

I had to tell him every detail. Then we watched tape. "What are you doing here?" he'd ask, referring to a receiver. He told me to run a hook route. He wanted to see if I would demonstrate the proper technique. Did I know what I was talking about? Chuck was going to find out. Chuck Noll was one of the smartest men I've ever met in my life. He could coach all the positions on the team probably better than the position coaches. Plus, when I got there, he was also the special teams coach.

Interview over, and after sending me on my way, Chuck waited a while to make a decision. Finally, George went into his office and asked, "Chuck, what are you going to do?" He said, "Well, I haven't quite made up my mind yet, but I think I know which way I'm going." And George said, "Well, do this. Hire Tom Moore and if you don't like him at the end of the year, you can fire me and him."

Chuck called me and brought me to the Steelers. I owe George Perles for helping me live my dream.

I was one of six assistant coaches on the Pittsburgh staff, three on offense and three on defense—not an uncommon setup in those days.

If you want to talk about the evolution of the NFL, let's start at the size of the coaching staffs. When longtime coach Bruce

Arians returned to the NFL with the Buccaneers, he brought me and a lot of his former assistants to Tampa Bay with him. Including trainers, we had twenty-nine people on the Bucs staff that won Super Bowl LV in February 2021.

On the Steelers in 1977, we had Dick Hoak, Rollie Dotsch, and me in the offensive coaches' office.

Dick Hoak had been a great running back for Penn State before playing ten years with the Steelers. After his playing career ended, he coached a year in high school and then Chuck brought him back to coach running backs. He would also go on to coach with Bill Cowher. He gets credit for Franco, and later doing the same thing for Jerome Bettis.

Dick had a great demeanor and a great ability and knack for teaching. It was just the way he did it. Of course, he had played running back at Penn State and with the Steelers for ten years. He had experienced it, and he would teach them the proper techniques and fundamentals. What to look for. How to handle blocking techniques, pass protection. Route running with backs coming out of the backfield. He had a great way of communicating with those guys and getting the best out of them.

Chuck was low-key, Dick was more laid-back than Chuck, and I've never been one to talk much.

One time, Rollie was gone or something. I said to George Perles, "I'm not going to say anything and see how long it takes for Dick to say something to me." We went about two and a half days without speaking. Finally, our linebacker coach, Woody Widenhofer, said to Dick, "You don't talk very much, do you?" And Dick said, "Every time I listen to you, I know I'm right, so there's nothing to talk about."

. . .

BY THE TIME I got to the Steelers, the team had already won two Super Bowls. But as I mentioned, those Terrible Towels the team's radio color commentator Myron Cope created didn't wave for the offense.

Before Chuck Noll arrived and started winning Lombardi Trophies, Buddy Parker, who had coached the Steelers from 1957 to 1964 and even brought quarterback Bobby Layne with him from Detroit, said he believed the Steelers would one day have good fortune and that it would last for fifty years. That prediction has held up pretty well.

A lot of the Steelers' success had to do with the 1974 draft. Pittsburgh's first round pick was Southern Cal receiver Lynn Swann. The second-round pick was Kent State linebacker Jack Lambert. They didn't have a third rounder. Receiver John Stallworth from Alabama A&M was the fourth rounder, and Wisconsin center Mike Webster was the fifth rounder. It's arguably the best draft of all time with four Hall of Fame players taken with the Steelers' first four picks. (Safety Donnie Shell, also a future Hall of Famer, was signed as an undrafted free agent at the end of the 1974 draft.)

It may have helped that 1974 was a strike year in the NFL. Players were challenging the Rozelle Rule, named after commissioner Pete Rozelle, which limited player movement through free agency. The veterans missed most of training camp, so that gave Chuck an opportunity to work with a lot of free agents and the new draft picks. Chuck—the ultimate teacher—helped four or five of those undrafted free agents make the team and become full-time contributors. Safety Donnie Shell, defensive end John Banaszak, and tight end Randy Grossman were all undrafted free agents.

The two figures credited most often for the Steelers' turn-around (the team was 1–13, 5–9, and 6–8 in '69, '70 and '71, respectively) were Chuck Noll and defensive tackle Joe Greene. Coincidentally, they arrived in Pittsburgh one day apart. Noll was hired on January 27, 1969, and Greene was drafted by the Steelers the next day.

He was "Mean" Joe Greene before he got to the Steelers. The nickname followed him from North Texas, which is known as the "Mean Green." At 6' 4", 275 pounds, Joe had intimidating size and strength. He was a violent player. He had a wide back and huge hands. But with all that size also came great balance and agility.

Those were the days before weightlifting really became prevalent in the NFL. I think a few years before Joe retired, we had a player named Steve Courson from South Carolina. He developed a heart problem after becoming one of the first NFL players to acknowledge using steroids. He was a big weightlifter. We were in training camp, and after the first day watching Courson, Joe said, "Whoo. I think I'd better get back in that weight room!"

Joe was the leader of the Steel Curtain, the Steelers defensive front that included Dwight White, Ernie Holmes, and L. C. Greenwood.

Joe took ownership of the team and after '74 so did Jack Lambert. When those two guys spoke, everybody listened. Lambert wasn't that big. He weighed 216 or 217, but he could run. To protect him, they put Joe in the gap. If the center tried to reach Joe, he had no chance. He was too fast. He was gone. If they blocked down and tried to pull the center to Lambert, he was gone. The premise of the whole thing was protecting Jack. It made Jack proficient, but he was a really, really great football player. You talk about a guy intrinsically motivated. That was Jack.

JACK'S SELF-MOTIVATION reminds me that in my role with Tampa Bay, I was asked by Bucs then-offensive coordinator Dave Canales to address the team with important coaching points during organized team activities (OTAs). Rookies need to hear these things, but they are good reminders to veterans as well. So, I put together a little outline from my decades of coaching in the NFL with guys such as Chuck Noll, Tony Dungy, Bruce Arians, and others. You'll see three kinds of Coaching Points—"Things You Have to Guard Against," "Five Football Essentials," and "Myths of Football." These are the sidebars throughout the book. On the next page, you'll see the first one.

ON THE STEELERS' OFFENSE, the leader was Mike Webster. Terry Bradshaw had enough to do as the quarterback, and Franco Harris was fairly soft-spoken. But the bigger the game, the greater the game Franco played. He was a five-star player. People would get upset with him because sometimes he would run out of bounds and things like that. He didn't take any unnecessary hits.

When it was time to go, he'd go. And he was deceptively fast. He was a fullback, but we ran two split backs. Rocky Bleier did the blocking when we ran to the weak side, and Rocky was a really good blocker.

You see, there are three ways you run the ball: 1)You find the hole. That's Barry Sanders. You give him the ball and he finds a hole. That's the zone blocking scheme. 2) You create a hole, where you double-team down and kick out for a lead through the hole. Well, that wasn't Barry Sanders because that has to happen when you get there. You have to trust the hole will be there. 3) You run with finesse. That's the option where the quarterback can elect to run the ball or pitch it to the running back. And we're not going to do that. There's the finesse aspect to the option, sure, but your quarterback is exposed to the defense, and quarterbacks don't last in a demolition derby.

Our line at Pittsburgh, we weren't that big by NFL standards. We weren't going to zone block and knock people off the ball. But we were going to double-team and trap, double-team and lead up—and that's what we did. Mike Webster wasn't that fast. But he'd been a wrestler at Wisconsin. And wrestlers are tremendous because they learn balance and leverage.

The Steelers' running backs were the biggest part of Noll's offense. In 1976, Franco and Rocky each rushed for 1,000 yards, and it was only a 14-game season.

COACHING POINTS

FIVE FOOTBALL ESSENTIALS

▶ *We're Here to Teach, Not Motivate You*

Motivation comes from learning so you can be successful. Chuck Noll used to tell the team at the first meeting, "I'm here to teach you, not motivate you. If I've got to motivate you, I've got to fire you." Chuck used to tell players that when it's the middle of the fourth quarter and we're asking you to do something, I'm not on the field with you and your position coach is up in the press box. So, you better motivate yourself.

Franco Harris, he wasn't just a great running back. He was clutch. The bigger the game, the greater he played. He was a really laid-back guy, and to me, one of the things that led to Franco's greatness was his coach Dick Hoak, who knew the running game like nobody I'd ever seen before. He had played the position, and he could really teach. He had a quiet demeanor, and like Franco he was from Penn State. He was such a great influence on Franco, and Franco trusted him so much to teach him the right technique, from route running to blitz pickup.

COACHING POINTS

THINGS YOU HAVE TO GUARD AGAINST

▶ *Bitching*

In my personal opinion, Bruce Arians did the most fantastic job of anybody during the pandemic year because I never heard one person, coach or player, bitch about anything. And the trip to Carolina was the trip from hell.

But we got there late, went out there and we beat them, and won eight straight. So quit your bitching.

As great as Franco was, I give a lot of credit to Dick Hoak and his coaching of Franco.

Of course, in those days we practiced on the game field at Three Rivers Stadium and all we had was 45 yards of playing field because we didn't practice where the baseball infield was for the Pittsburgh Pirates games. But every single play that Franco ran in practice, he'd run 40 yards and score a touchdown. We'd wait for him to come back, but that was his thing. Try to score on every play.

The guy that used to get Franco going was Joe Greene. Joe knew when guys needed a little extra kick. The great teams I've been involved with, the players have taken ownership of that team. With the Colts, it was Peyton Manning. With the Steelers, it was Joe Greene. Of course, with the Bucs it was Tom Brady. You need two or three ignitors per team, but you can't designate them. Now, I've been on other teams where the leadership was bad leadership, and they were always bitching and complaining. That happens, too, and it's something you've got to fight against.

As they say, coaching is simple, but it ain't easy.

It helps to have talent, and a lot of that was discovered by Bill Nunn Jr., one of the Steelers scouts and a tremendous individual. He took care of the Southwestern Athletic Conference and

Mid-Eastern Athletic Conference, made up of historically Black colleges. A lot of those guys were there with the Steelers because of Bill Nunn, Jr.

He probably had as much to do with the Steelers' greatness as anybody. His dad owned the *Courier*, which was a weekly newspaper in Pittsburgh. And when he got out of college, he was the sportswriter for it. For seventeen years he had selected the annual Black Colleges All America football team for the *Courier*. Each year, Bill also orchestrated that the top forty-four SWAC and MEAC conference players come to the Hilton for a banquet in Pittsburgh.

In his column, Bill Nunn was fast to point out that the Steelers were not investing much time or effort in scouting Black football programs.

Supposedly, Dan Rooney came over and asked Bill Jr., "Do you think you can help us?" He said yes, but he didn't want to work there full-time at first, keeping his column with the *Courier*.

The Steelers had drafted more players from those traditionally Black colleges after Nunn joined them in 1969. He helped them land stars such as Stallworth, Mel Blount, L. C. Greenwood, Donnie Shell, and Joe Gilliam. In 1974, Gilliam became the first African American quarterback to start a season opener since the NFL-AFL merger.

Football and race—like most things in America—have a complicated history, and I've witnessed it evolve over the decades I've been coaching. But I was blessed from a young age with experiences, relationships, and fatherly advice that put me on the right path regarding race and respect.

When the Second World War started, my family moved to Mt. Pleasant, Iowa, and my father got a job at the Iowa

Ordnance Plant in Middletown, Iowa, where they made ammunition and bombs for the military. We moved from one house to another. We got one home from a guy who owned a farm, and we were right next to a predominately Black neighborhood. The guys who lived there became my friends and they were everything I had, and everybody I knew. I became good friends with a guy named Paschal Bennett. He and I took a lot of heat. This is back in 1942–43. I can remember kids at school called me a lot of names. They called me white trash and stuff like that. Of course, they called him a lot of disparaging names. One of the first lessons I learned during this time was from my dad. With my friend being called a lot of different names, I asked my father, "How do I refer to him?" He said, "Do you have a name?" I said, "Yeah, my name is Tom Moore." He said, "Does he have a name?" I said, "Yeah, it's Paschal Bennett." He said, "Well then, call him Paschal; that's his name." He taught me not to call anybody anything except their names. And don't call anyone by their nickname. Sometimes nicknames are given to people for the wrong reasons, and they're offensive. Call people by their first name and give them respect.

Respect was a big thing with my dad. One time I made the horrible mistake of calling my mother a liar. Before I knew it, I was disciplined by my father. From then on, I may have told my mother, "I'm not sure you got that story quite right," but I never called her a liar again.

Another lesson learned from my father was about dealing with the racism. He told me to call people by their name and when they ask you your race, you tell them you're a member of the human race. Everywhere I've been, many of my friends are Black. I've always felt very comfortable with everyone.

And I once made a connection with a true pioneer with regard to race and the gridiron. If you watch a game at the University of Iowa, you will see Duke Slater Field, which they named in 2021. (The stadium at Iowa is Kinnick Stadium. It's named after their Heisman Trophy winner from 1939, Nile Kinnick.) Duke Slater, who played tackle from 1918 to 1921, was the first Black athlete at Iowa. He also was a four-time first-team All Pro with the Rock Island Independents and Chicago Cardinals and was named to the Pro Football Hall of Fame's Centennial Class in 2020. Slater later became a judge in Chicago. He was a wonderful man. The Iowa Club had a big all-sports banquet at the end of the year when I was a student athlete there, and my job was to get a speaker, and I got Duke Slater to speak at it. I even went to Chicago and spent a couple of days with him.

THERE'S ONE THING I learned in graduate school, and I used it in recruiting, that has been a reason why I've had some success in coaching. I've seen recruiters visit players at their homes or schools and jump right into promises, promises, promises. But there was a guidance and counseling course I took that taught me to take a different approach. Before you tell a potential player what you can do, ask him what he's looking for. Then, you'll know what to talk about. It's the same with coaching. You should ask the players, "What's your vision? Where do you want to go?" Then, talk to them. If you don't know what they're looking for, anything you offer that doesn't hit the mark can come off as disrespectful or even offensive. There's a saying that players don't care how much you know until they know you care. I think that's true. Once a player

COACHING POINTS

FIVE FOOTBALL ESSENTIALS

▶ Know What to Do

That's classroom. That's watching the tape. John McKay said anything is simple if you understand it. He said, "I understand the pitch sweep, but Einstein doesn't have a clue. Einstein knows the Theory of Relativity, and I don't have the first idea how it works. So, you've got to make it simple."

knows you're in his corner, he will listen. People want people on their side.

The first player on the Steelers to come in and meet me was Lynn Swann. He was already a first-round draft pick, a Super Bowl MVP, and recognized as one of the best receivers in the NFL. I was his new position coach, coming from college at the University of Minnesota and replacing an incredibly popular receivers coach in Lionel Taylor, who had also played receiver in the NFL.

I can imagine Lynn Swann wanting to see how this college coach was going to make him and John Stallworth better.

Lynn was (and continues to be) very personable and polished, with a big smile. He came in and said, "Tom, this is a good team and John Stallworth and I, we can catch the football. We don't need a lot of work on catching drills." But then he said, "John and I want to be great at this game. We want to make some money, which you can at this game, and we want to play a long time. So, as a suggestion, teach us what we don't know to help us become great."

Of course, I already knew they were great players. I said, "Well, what don't you know?" He said, "We're not really sure on route adjustments, reading coverages, adjusting to those coverages, making sure we get in the right place."

So, that's what we worked on. And when we threw individual routes to Swann and Stallworth and the other receivers, oh, probably 40 percent of the time, we threw against double coverage. How do you beat double coverage? That's what we worked on because those guys were going to get it.

A good example of how to beat double coverage is a play we used to beat the Los Angeles Rams in Super Bowl XIV. You'll hear about it again later, but it was called 60 Prevent Slot Hook and Go.

That was our answer in the Super Bowl with John Stallworth. We knew he was going to get double coverage. We knew they were going to go in and out on John, so we diagrammed how he'd come off the ball, and once he read the double coverage, he ran an in cut and then a post route right past Rams defensive back Rod Perry.

Terry Bradshaw delivered the ball away from Perry, over the opposite shoulder John was expecting. He made the adjustment and the play resulted in a 73-yard touchdown in our 31–19 win over the Rams.

That's one way to beat the double coverage.

When you get a defense that will play one defender short and the other long, where one defender plays underneath the receiver and another defender plays over the top, you need to get beyond the first defender to get him in the trail position. Then you've got to give him misdirection and shake him one way while you go the other way. Those are just two methods, and we drilled them and drilled them and drilled them.

John Elway once said, to be great, you've got to be good every day. That's all you have to do. Be good every day and you will become great.

I believe there are six points that can hinder people's progress: greed, jealousy, boredom, death by inches, bitching, or complaining and agendas. To climb the stairs from good to being great, one of the biggest things you have to fight is boredom. Repetition can induce boredom. But it's got to be repetition day after day after day after day after day in order to get better. Some people can't do that; they get weary. Before they accomplish perfection in one thing, they want to move on to the next thing. You have to fight the boredom of the continual repetition of doing things right all the time. Be good every day.

ALL THIS STUFF about fights and being good triggers a memory of my childhood. Little Tom Moore had a stuttering problem. Between my best friend Paschal being Black and me stuttering, a lot of people made fun of us, so we had a lot of fights. I think it was through all those fights that I met one of my guardian angels, my art teacher Beverly Carpenter. She befriended me because my father, at this particular time, was working on the railroad and the only time he came home was Saturday morning. He was there Saturday and he left again on Sunday. He was what they called a Gandy dancer, the people who worked on the railroad and lived in a boxcar. They had one boxcar that served as a living room and kitchen, and another boxcar had bunk beds where they slept.

He was part of a crew of eight. They parked the boxcar on a side track and were responsible for keeping the tracks going and making repairs. He wasn't home often, but when he did come home, he taught me some lessons that needed to be learned. Number one was work. We raised our own food, except for meat and milk, things like that. But we raised all our vegetables—tomatoes, potatoes. My mother canned stuff. He worked and my mother was a nurse. She used to get up at three in the morning and made eight pies every day for the restaurant in town where she dropped them off on the way to work so my brother and I could eat there.

My art teacher was concerned about me fighting all the time. I got into a lot of fights. But I had to.

I'll never forget, Mrs. Carpenter had gotten married. She said, "I'll make you a deal, Tom. You stop fighting for a month and my husband and I will take you to an outdoor drive-in theater to watch a movie and we'll buy you a present." I said, "That's a pretty good deal." A month went by, and she said, "Okay, let's go buy something." We got it at a porcelain place. It was a piggy bank shaped like a football. We went to the theater and watched the drive-in movie. I can't remember the film, but after we came home that night and she dropped me off at my house, I couldn't sleep.

I remember that because about two weeks prior to doing this, I had gotten into a fight, and I didn't tell her

COACHING POINTS

FIVE FOOTBALL ESSENTIALS

▶ *Know How to Do It*

Technique. Fundamentals. Teaching. Know how to do something. If you know what to do and how to do it, you can play fast. If you play fast, you can play harder, longer than the next guy. Eventually you break a person's will. I can show you in the Super Bowl, the Chiefs had fourth-and-8 on about our 16-yard line. Patrick Mahomes rolls to his right and Will Gholston chases him down and trips him up a little bit and he threw an incomplete pass. We were up two scores at that time. If they go and score, it's a game. But they didn't and that was it.

You break their will. But you can't do that if you can't play fast. And you can't play fast if you don't know exactly what you're doing. It's like I told these new guys. I know exactly how to get to the airport. You kind of know. I will beat you there every time. Now if you know and I know, now it's a race—but I know which lane to get into at which time. That's my edge.

about it. I felt so bad and had such a conscience attack that I lay awake until dawn.

Then, I went to her house and knocked on the door and gave her the bank back. And you know, I respect her to this day. She didn't say, "That's okay, Tom. Keep the bank." She took the bank back and I never did get the bank. That was cool. That was okay. She said, "Tom, you've got to stop that. You've got to grow up. You've got to leave things alone. You can't do that." She really nurtured me and took care of me, and she taught me a thing or two about basic principles and discipline that I'd see later in life working with Chuck Noll.

FOR THE THIRTEEN YEARS I was at training camp with Chuck Noll, who believed in teaching fundamentals and techniques, we spent the first hour of the first camp practice teaching how to block and how to tackle by the numbers.

We walked through and then we picked up the pace. And we taught these blocking and tackling basics, these essentials for an intense sixty minutes. We taught *everybody*. We taught the offensive players how to tackle in case we got into a situation where we'd thrown an interception or fumbled or those guys were playing special teams. You've got to know how to tackle.

You've got the defensive players. They had to know how to block, too. A lot of those guys were on special teams. Or if you get an interception or recover a fumble on defense, you want to be prepared to block for your teammate.

Chuck was so thorough, and it was every year. It didn't make a difference how long you'd played. There were no exceptions. Joe Greene was out there his last year going through a walk-through, step-by-step, working through it. Mike Webster played a long time, but his final year, I guarantee you, the first day of practice he was working on blocking and tackling by the numbers.

Then, after an hour of basic learning, we had the *application* of it. We went to what they call the Oklahoma Drill with the linemen and the linebackers. It was one-on-one blocking with the back running behind the blocker through the hole made by two dummies, one on each side.

The wide receivers and defensive backs were on the other field working on pass routes and coming off the line of scrimmage and the techniques of blocking.

Obviously, you've got to have the God-given ability. But after you have that, you've got to be willing to pay the price to perfect your talent. That's very hard. It's very long and it's very laborious. Some people can do it because they don't get bored.

You never really get accomplished to the level you want. You can always improve. You see guys like Peyton Manning. I wasn't there for his last game at Denver. But I know in the thirteen years at Indianapolis, he prepared for every last game exactly like he prepared for the first game of his career.

In the offseason, Peyton, the quarterback coach, and I would start the second Monday in March. We'd go four days a week. We'd start at 6:30 a.m. and go through all the game tapes play-by-play. We'd go through the interception reel. We'd go through the touchdown reel. We'd go through the sack reel. What caused those things? Peyton would make notes going through all these tapes; he was making a list of what he felt he personally needed to work on.

We'd go over the list and he'd say, "Hey, Tom, in OTAs [organized team activities] and minicamp, here's what I need to work on to get better."

COACHING POINTS

THINGS YOU HAVE TO GUARD AGAINST

▶ *Boredom*

I tell them we start the seventeenth of April and finish hopefully sometime in the middle of February. That's a long time. You've got to fight boredom. Coaches have to fight boredom. So, coaches, here's what happens sometimes. Coaches are very insecure; we don't think we're doing a good job unless we put in four new plays and three new passes. Well, if you put them in, you've got to run them. You've got to practice them. Then, all of a sudden, the first of November, all that shit you did the first of September, you ain't doing it anymore. If that shit is so good in November, why didn't we do it in September, Coach? You've got to fight boredom.

Lynn Swann and John Stallworth were both great at that. They would say, "Let's do the things we're having trouble with to master this. We know some things. We can do some things and we'll keep working on those. But let's emphasize the things we're having difficulty with and master those things."

I just happened to hear how Mavericks guard Kyrie Irving won a game shooting a shot left-handed. He was talking about how he practices that particular shot a half hour or forty-five minutes a week. As a coach, your responsibility is to do what you have to do to give those guys an opportunity to be the very best they can be.

That involves setting up study plans for them. That involves setting up drills for them. That involves watching tape with them and going over things so you're constantly making corrections.

Like I tell people, when you think you can't get any better is when you start to tail off.

I'm a firm believe that no matter how good you are, you can always get better. Now, the guys that get better are the guys who *work* on it. To me, that's the fun of coaching. That's why I love to coach—because you're helping these guys. To be a great receiver, you've got to have a great quarterback. To be a great quarterback, you've got to have great receivers. I understand that. But from a coaching standpoint, it's your job to get all those pieces together.

At the professional level, I insisted on the same things I had done at the University of Minnesota. I'd start with the techniques and fundamentals, as basic as getting in your stance. How to come off the football. Blocking. Tackling. Rinse, repeat. Over and over again.

Would that kind of coaching work in the NFL? I had some concerns until I met Chuck and quickly discovered he was all about teaching the basics, the fundamentals.

And it turns out that I wasn't the only one who had concerns about this kind of coaching. When I left the University of Minnesota, knowing how hard I coached them and all my rules, I think my former players had a pool on how long I would last with the Steelers.

Tony Dungy probably tells it the best.

"I got a great story about Tom, too, and his adaptability and doing what players needed and that came from Coach Noll," Dungy said. "Coach Noll told us our job was to help our players but when Tom left Minnesota to go to the Steelers, our whole offensive group is sitting there saying, 'How long do you think he's going to last there?' Guys are saying three months. Six months. No way he can coach those guys like he coached us. At Minnesota, we couldn't wear long-sleeved shirts. No gloves. He was yelling at guys. Yeah, six months. That's the maximum they gave him.

"But when I get there the next year as an undrafted free agent, he's definitely changed. He's still Tom, but he figured it out. This isn't the biggest thing in the world. To us college kids, though, it was. For those guys on the Steelers, it's not. He figured out what those guys needed."

But I had some learning to do. My first big mistake came in the first preseason game. I still had a college coach's mindset, and of course in college, you lose one game and you've got a pretty good chance of not winning the national championship. We played every game to win. My first year with the Steelers, we were playing a preseason game against Buffalo. Back in those days, you played six preseason games, and the starters played the first quarter, then we'd play the reserves, the backups. We're late in the game and Buffalo is beating us, 24–21.

Stallworth and Swann had been sitting out the entire second quarter, the entire third quarter, and most of the fourth quarter.

Thanks to me and my desire not to lose, we get the two-minute warning and I put Stallworth and Swann back in the game. I didn't know it at the time, but that's a real, real no-no, especially in the NFL. You don't want to risk getting your best players injured to win a game that doesn't count. You get them in the game, let them get some work, and hopefully get them out before anything bad happens.

After the game, the other Steelers assistants informed me and said, "Hey, Tom, don't do that again." But we won the game, 28–24.

Lesson learned. It's funny. There's plenty of people who say preseason doesn't mean anything. Well, you lose about three of them in a row, and I'll show you how much they mean. I remember George Perles telling Chuck, "I want to get everybody in the game. We're going to win this game because I've been here when we lost preseason games and that ain't worth it. We come up here, you're grumpy, I'm grumpy, everybody's grumpy. So to hell with that. It doesn't make any difference; we're going to win it."

Chuck was Chuck, not one for a lot of rah-rah speeches or chatter.

We all feared him a little bit. One Christmas, some of the players decided to go to the upper St. Clair neighborhood where some players lived and sing Christmas carols. One of them said, "Let's stop by Chuck's house." The others said, "I don't know if that's a good idea." They stopped anyway, and Chuck came out and was caroling with them.

Anyway, we started having real success in the passing game, throwing the ball more than the team had in previous years. Terry—now in his eighth season—was really coming on. And the rule changes helped. Before '78, nobody could get off the line of scrimmage across from Mel Blount except for one guy—the Raiders' Cliff Branch. He didn't get off often. For our receivers, being free from contact after five yards opened things up a lot. In fact, I thought I might give receiving a shot—well, at least in practice.

You see, back in those days, you had a minicamp Memorial Day weekend. The quarterbacks came in early, and we'd meet in the morning and go out on the field after lunch and let the quarterbacks throw a little bit just so they could get the feel of throwing the football. The coaches would be the ones running routes. One day, I did an in-cut and my knee gave out as Bradshaw threw me a pass. I'd torn cartilage in my knee.

Football, even at a holiday weekend minicamp, is a violent game.

In the 1976 season opener, Raiders defensive back George Atkinson had put a huge hit on Swann. Chuck Noll told reporters the day after the game that Atkinson's hit was made with the intent to maim. And then Chuck went on to speak about "a criminal element" in the NFL. That was enough for Atkinson to sue Noll for slander in a civil court in Oakland.

Now, the Raiders and Steelers were already bitter rivals. This whole thing took it to another level. The first day of training camp, and our head coach is in court facing off against Atkinson, Raiders managing partner Al Davis, head coach John Madden, and more. It was an ugly ten-day trial, but the jury ultimately decided that there was no slander, no malice, and no damages for Atkinson.

I arrived at Saint Vincent College in Latrobe, Pennsylvania, for my first training camp with the Steelers and Chuck was in this lawsuit. So, it was up to us assistant coaches to get some work done.

The first week we had rookies, free agents, and guys coming off injured reserve. We spent a week working with those guys in double sessions. Bud Carson—our defensive coordinator—ran the show.

Nothing was scripted. When Tony Dungy joined the coaching staff after his playing days ended, he was in his first half-hour meeting before we got on the field, and he looked at me and whispered, "Tom, where's the practice schedule?" I said, "We don't have a practice schedule."

We'd do individual drills, then we'd go to group work and then team. Chuck Noll wanted teaching.

In training camp, it was us against us, so there was no script. The offense just calls the plays, and the defense has to call their plays. Then, when we got to the season, Hoak used to run the scout team against the defense, and we used 3 x 5 index cards. He'd hold up these little 3 x 5 cards to show everyone the plays and now we have these big, laminated sheets all printed out.

Chuck would tell George, "Give us some Cover 1, mix in some Cover 2 and Cover 3." It was improvisation. That way, you had to process things on the fly.

In the game, it's the same. You have to adjust to the defense or offense, process everything like you did in practice.

One method I used at training camp was to learn our own defensive playbook. I needed to make our receivers know exactly what our defense was doing, what they were thinking, what their technique was. Chuck found out and said, "What are you doing?" I said, "I'm looking at the defensive playbook." He said, "Tom, yes, you've got to tell them what the Cover 3 does. But they've got to process it on full speed."

The great receivers can process how they're supposed to beat a defensive coverage right after they leave the line of scrimmage.

Lynn was talking about recognizing and processing the coverage on the run and then executing. That's all about understanding the reception area, that window between defenders where the ball is going to be delivered. Fast-forward to a recent case in point. I'm coaching with the Bucs in 2023, we're playing Green Bay, and we had to win the game. The Packers went Cover 2. Okay, it's Cover 2 and you're the inside receiver and you've got a seam route. You're running off that safety. Once you beat him, your reception area is 18 yards deep, 2 yards outside the hashmarks. The pass that Baker Mayfield

COACHING POINTS

THINGS YOU HAVE TO GUARD AGAINST

▶ *Greed*

What's the other guy making? I get a kick out of these guys. They say, "I love the game. I love to coach and play. I love the competition. But I have to be the highest-paid coach or player." If I were a GM, I'd say, "Get the fuck out of here." It's all bullshit. That's probably why I've never been asked to GM.

threw to Chris Godwin on that route was perfect. And there was only 2 yards for him to catch it. If he hadn't been there, it's an interception.

It was a small window. If Godwin doesn't understand the importance of the reception window, it's an incompletion.

I guarantee you when Chris caught that pass, he was motivated. That's what coaching is about in the NFL. When you teach players how to do it and they have success, they're motivated. That was Chuck's philosophy. It wasn't about speeches. Knowledge and technique resulting in success is motivation.

We didn't have pep talks and all that shit. With pep talks, you've got to do it every day, and you just can't do it every day. You need players who are intrinsically motivated. Sometimes players lose their motivation based on why they're playing. Are they playing for the fame? Is it to make money?

Chuck Noll's definition of motivation was teaching someone how to do something that they didn't know how to do and having them do it with success. That's what motivates players: teaching them something that helps them excel on the field. Then they're motivated to learn more. The head coaches I worked for—Chuck Noll, Tony Dungy, Bruce Arians, and Todd Bowles among them—they all did a good job at the beginning of each week explaining to the players what we had to do to win the game. But it's always just a brief overview of what it's going to take. The real motivation takes place when the coaches teach the fundamentals and techniques essential to that particular game plan. That's what wins the game.

The NFL game is sophisticated. There's no room for error.

4

Chuck Noll
and His Life's Work

TWO HOURS BEFORE KICKOFF against the Houston Oilers in a 1989 wildcard game, I walked into the Steelers coaches' locker room at the Astrodome and saw Chuck Noll was sitting on a bench reading a book. Chuck always had a lot of interests outside of football. If he wanted to do something, he would pour himself into it and learn everything there was to learn.

"What are you reading, Chuck?" I asked him.

"I'm reading how to navigate my boat just by the stars," he said.

I waited a couple minutes, leaving him with his book. And then I asked, "What if it's cloudy?"

Chuck just looked at me and rolled his eyes.

That was Chuck. He didn't feel any pressure about coaching in a playoff game because he was completely prepared. Chuck led us to an overtime win against the Oilers that day with Gary Anderson kicking the winning field goal in overtime.

George Perles and I had a connection with Chuck because he'd played at Dayton, where we had coached under John McVay many years later.

Chuck was an undersized offensive lineman and linebacker who was drafted 239th overall by the Cleveland Browns in 1953. Head coach Paul Brown would use him as a messenger guard to run plays into the huddle. Chuck was quiet but tenacious and obviously well-coached. He had the pleasure of blocking for Jim Brown and Bobby Mitchell.

When it was time to "get on with his life's work," a phrase Chuck would take from Paul Brown, it was coaching.

Chuck had attended law school, but his heart was in football. He tried to get a coaching job at Dayton, but they didn't think he had enough coaching experience, so he went to the pros.

And he had some pretty good coaching influences. Not only did he play for Paul Brown, but he also coached with Sid Gilman and the Chargers of the American Football League. He was the defensive coordinator on Don Shula's Baltimore Colts' staff that lost Super Bowl III to Broadway Joe Namath and the New York Jets.

Before he came to the Steelers, he was a candidate for the Patriots head coaching job. But the Patriots didn't think their fan base would embrace a coach from the team that lost the Super Bowl—and lost as 19.5-point favorites—so they hired Clive Rush, a coach from the Jets staff that had won the whole thing.

In Pittsburgh, meanwhile, the Rooneys tried to talk Joe Paterno into leaving Penn State, but after he chose to remain with the Nittany Lions, the Steelers hired Chuck Noll. From Noll to Bill Cowher to Mike Tomlin, it's been nothing but historical success for the Steelers ever since.

In 1969, Chuck became the Steelers' fourth head coach in sixteen years. His first season with the Steelers, they went 1–13. They won their first game of the season 16–13 over the Lions, then proceeded to lose 13 in a row.

Mr. Rooney once told me he thought Chuck did his best job coaching the first year there when he was 1–13.

"Why would you say that?" I asked.

And Art replied, "He had a plan, he stuck to his plan, and he didn't lose the team."

It was like Jimmy Johnson's first year in Dallas, when he was 1–15. I remember telling Cowboys owner Jerry Jones that exact story. Jimmy went on to win two Super Bowls.

Chuck's big thing was teaching. Chuck used to tell us, "Pressure is being asked to do something you don't know how to do. If someone told me to perform heart surgery, that's pressure. But if you know what the hell you're doing, there's no pressure." Yes, there's the challenge of execution. But Chuck took the pressure off his players by teaching, not talking.

The Steelers' training camp at Saint Vincent College in Latrobe, Pennsylvania, was about forty miles from Pittsburgh. Back in those days, camp lasted nine weeks. We played 14 regular season games and 6 preseason games. Today, we play only 3 preseason games, and there are no two-a-day practices. Training camp—for the Buccaneers—is at the team's facility in Tampa, and players stay in a five-star hotel.

St. Vincent's was pretty Spartan. We had no air-conditioning. There was one pay phone at each end of the hallway. The players were in pads every day, twice a day.

After practice, the coaches and media that covered the team had what they called a "five o'clock club" in the administrative building. You'd go up there and they would have soda, beer, pretzels, and potato chips—whatever. Then you'd go to dinner.

You'd come back and meet from seven until ten. Then at ten, you'd go back to the "five o'clock club." At that late hour, they had some hard liquor and some wine and barbecue, grits and chicken and stuff. Eleven o'clock was curfew. If you wanted to go out, you could. But you can't do that now.

We were out there for nine weeks. That's enough time for someone to piss you off.

I never heard Chuck raise his voice to an assistant coach or player. I was there thirteen years. He never told me, "You did a good job." But he did tell me one time, "You're doing a good job, or you wouldn't be here." Chuck never needed anybody to pat him on the back to boost his ego, and he didn't expect others to need it, either. But I think some people do need it. That's how they function.

Terry Bradshaw was one of those people. I'll get into his complex relationship with Chuck later, but Terry captured a lot of it when he told me, "With Chuck, you were always on edge, which is good. I mean, obviously I can't complain. You get fucking tough playing for Chuck Noll."

THERE WERE A LOT OF CHUCKISMS—beliefs and sayings—that we all became used to.

For example, the offense taking a safety in a game when it would help finish the contest. Chuck absolutely refused to take a safety on offense.

When I became the coordinator, I was practicing taking a safety in case the situation presented itself in a game. Chuck asked, "What are you doing?"

I said, "I'm practicing taking a safety, Coach."

He said, "You can practice it all you want but we aren't going to ever do it. I'm not giving them any points."

Trips out west where jet lag, time differences, and more might be factors. . . . One time we were going to San Diego and a reporter asked Chuck, "What's your philosophy about going out west? Do you go two days early or one day early or what?"

Chuck, in a very nonchalant way, said, "I really don't care when we go. Just make sure Joe Greene is on the plane."

Then there's "first down, fall down" in the fourth quarter when you're up. You need a first down but then you should fall down in bounds (even if the end zone is within reach) to keep the clock running, move on to the next play, snap, and kneel—game over. Logically, that's the best thing to do. Chuck wasn't into that and, apparently, neither was I because it was tough for me to tell a guy not to score a touchdown.

When I was the offensive coordinator for the Colts, we were playing Kansas City at Arrowhead Stadium, and that particular situation came up. Running back Dominic Rhodes popped a play and went 80 yards for a touchdown and I caught all kinds of hell for that. But that's the way I was taught. If you can score a touchdown, score a touchdown. And Chuck's thing was, if the defense can't hold them, we don't deserve to win.

It gets even crazier, or so you would think. When Pittsburgh was playing Dallas in Super Bowl X, there was 1:28 remaining and the Steelers had the ball, leading 21–17. It was fourth-and-9 at the Dallas 41-yard line. Chuck went for it.

Now the real reason he went for it was that our punt protection was breaking down and he was worried about getting the punt blocked. So he gave the ball to Rocky Bleier, who gained only 2 yards. But on the sidelines, George Perles was in Chuck's ear, saying, "Chuck! Chuck! Punt it! Punt it, Chuck!"

Remember, this was the Super Bowl with the Dallas Cowboys and Roger Staubach. Chuck looked at George and said, "If we can't hold them, we don't deserve to win." That's how confident he was in the Steel Curtain. The Cowboys drove to the Pittsburgh 38-yard line before Glen Edwards sealed the win with an interception.

George Perles used to drive Chuck crazy. You know Myron Cope? Myron was the color commentator for Steelers games on radio for thirty-five years. He's the inventor of the Terrible Towel. He used to stir up stuff. On his radio show, Myron used to call Chuck "The Emperor."

In training camp, George would say, "You know, Chuck, it ain't easy working for an emperor." Chuck would say, "I ain't no damn emperor!" George said, "I don't know. Myron Cope calls you that every time I listen to the radio."

"Oh, screw Myron Cope!" Chuck shouted. Chuck was never a fan of those kinds of titles. He just really wanted to be known as Coach Noll.

CHUCK NOLL WAS THE BEST TEACHER I've ever been around. He left nothing to chance. He knew how to develop players.

We were coaching the South team at the Senior Bowl in 1982 and me and Dick Hoak were working on a mini playbook. Marv Levy and his Chiefs staff coached the North squad.

The Senior Bowl was coached by staffs whose teams didn't make the playoffs. They had been waiting for years to get Chuck Noll down there in Mobile, Alabama, and when we finished 8–8 in 1981 and missed the postseason, they jumped at the chance to invite us.

Chuck came by and asked me and Dick, "What are you doing?" We told him what we were drawing up. "Did you watch any tape yet?" he asked. We said, "No." He said, "Well, how in the hell can you make a playbook if you don't know what the hell they can do?" So he made us watch a couple days' worth of tape—footage of our South team players—before we got back to the playbook.

We had John Fourcade, the quarterback from Ole Miss. He was a dual threat, maybe more dangerous as a runner than he was a passer. He wasn't a pocket passer, but more of a sprint-out-type quarterback. He had 25 touchdown passes as a starter at Ole Miss and another 22 TDs on the ground. Dick Hoak and I put in a lot of sprint-outs, bootlegs, and nakeds. In fact, Fourcade would wind up being the game's MVP.

Cut to the game. Cut to halftime. Remember, the Senior Bowl is a showcase for players done with their college eligibility. But there I caught Chuck Noll teaching a guard from some small school, someone who was never going to play pro football, the techniques of the pressure G on the trap play. It's the Senior Bowl and here's Chuck coaching his ass off under the bleachers at halftime. You wouldn't believe he was the head coach of an NFL team that would win four Super Bowls. None of that mattered to Chuck. He saw a chance to help a player, even one from a small school who wasn't going to play in the NFL, and he felt it was his job to teach the kid.

There was a time when I bumped heads with Chuck on one of his ideas.

In 1977, the Steelers drafted Jim Smith, who had played flanker and wingback at Michigan. He was 6-foot-2, 215 pounds, and a great athlete. One day during the 1979 season, Chuck came to me and said, "I think we should get Jim Smith in the game more." There was no way I was going to take out Swann. I said, "No. Chuck, no. I can't do that. I can't justify it. I love Jim Smith and I know he's good, but I can't do that." They both played the right wide receiver position.

"Well," he said, "I want Jim Smith in there." I said, "He'll get in there some."

But Chuck had confronted me, and I knew I had to do something. On Monday, I went into Chuck's office and I said, "Let me propose something and see what you think." That was the best way to get something done with Chuck.

I said, "Let's do this. Bennie Cunningham is our tight end and a good blocker. He's a better blocker than a receiver. But instead of taking Swann or Stallworth out, let's substitute Bennie with Smith and go three wideouts, especially in two-minute situations and on third down. We've still got our two backs. Three wideouts. We've got our split ends on each side, and we've got a good receiver in the slot."

Chuck said, "That's a good idea." So Jim was our slot receiver on passing downs. That way Jim was getting 20 or 25 snaps a game, playing time he deserved. We used him mostly on third down and in our two-minute offense. And that was probably the closest I ever came to not seeing eye-to-eye with Chuck.

It helped that Swann bailed me out with a spectacular game. Not just a good game, a *spectacular* game. He caught 5 passes for 192 yards and 2 touchdowns in a 37–17 win over the Bengals.

You have to adapt to your talent, and that's what Chuck did the best. Some coaches have a preconceived notion of what they want to do when they get a head coaching job.

You see all these head coaching openings and a candidate will interview for a job and bring his offense and say, "This is what we do." A new coach might meet with his staff and team and say, "This is what we want to do."

Both bad ideas. You should do what your players can do. That's one of the things that made Bill Walsh so great. He took what Joe Montana could do and he designed an offense to maximize Joe Montana and his ability. It carried over with Steve Young. Here's what Joe Montana can do. Here's what Steve Young does best. Let's do that.

When you're a coach and you go in for an interview and your potential employer asks you what kind of offense you're going to run, you say, "Well, I know this offense, I know that offense. But I'm going to watch tape and I'm going to see what our players can do, and I'll make an offense that takes advantage of what our people do best." You know, that's your job as a coach, to maximize the abilities of the players you have.

Then there's the stats and rankings. When I was at Indianapolis in 2008, we won the last 9 games. Then we lost in the playoffs to San Diego in overtime. The next year, we ran off 14 straight wins. So we won 23 regular season games in a row, which is still the NFL record.

COACHING POINTS

MYTHS OF FOOTBALL

▶ *You Can't Win Three Times Against the Same Team in One Season.*

That's bullshit because it's been done before. New Orleans thought it was true. In 2020 with the Bucs, we lost to them twice in the regular season and then beat them in the NFC divisional game. They bought into that myth.

I got Peyton Manning, one of the greatest quarterbacks to ever play the game. Marvin Harrison will be joined by Reggie Wayne in the Pro Football Hall of Fame. We had Dallas Clark. Joseph Addai.

I had some extremely skilled people and we won a lot of games . . . *and we were thirty-second in rushing.* Instead of talking about the 23 games we won, sportswriters would say, "I see where you're thirty-second in rushing." You think I care? Really? The object of the game is to win. It's not to tally stats. People say the team's stats aren't good enough? Shit. . . . When somebody gets fired, the first thing ownership, media, fans, *everybody* will tell you is you didn't win enough games.

The goal of the game is to win. I think of Iowa coach Kirk Ferentz when he went 10–2 in 2023 and people blasted him for not scoring as many points as they thought the team should've scored. To hell with that. What's important is winning. I think he did a great job of coaching because he took a defense and punter and won ten games.

There are a lot of ways to skin a cat. Chuck Noll certainly understood this.

The Steelers' first two Super Bowl teams won with the Steel Curtain defense and giving the football to running backs Franco Harris and Rocky Bleier.

January 1975, Super Bowl IX against the Vikings was played on a frigid day at Tulane Stadium in New Orleans. Franco Harris rushed for 158 yards on 34 carries, was voted Most Valuable Player, and the Steelers won 16–6. Bradshaw only attempted 14 passes in the game, completing 9 for 96 yards and a touch-down. The defense only gave up 21 yards rushing in the Vikings' 17 attempts. Chuck rode off on the shoulders of Joe Greene and Franco, who had carried the team further than they did the head coach that day.

Bradshaw played a bigger role in the Steelers' 21–17 win over Dallas next year in Super Bowl X at the Orange Bowl. He still only completed 9 passes in 19 attempts, but he threw for 209 yards, 2 TDs, and no interceptions. In those days, only five starting quarterbacks completed at least 60 percent of their passes, so completing about half of your attempts was more the norm. Lynn Swann, who caught 4 passes for 161 yards and a touchdown, was named the game's MVP. His juggling, highlight-reel catch of a 64-yard bomb over Cowboys defensive back Mark Washington is still the stuff of legends.

Steelers defensive back Mel Blount was so physical at the line of scrimmage with receivers, and they lost so many beatings, that the NFL changed its pass coverage rules in 1978 to outlaw bump-and-run coverage down the field.

Fast-forward to 1978 and the implementation of the Mel Blount Rule. That was the year after I arrived in Pittsburgh. Terry Bradshaw was up to using those rules to our advantage.

"It was totally out of character for us," Bradshaw said of becoming a passing team.

But with the bump-and-run outlawed, Bradshaw and his receivers were going to let it fly. It had been two years since the Steelers last appeared in a Super Bowl and the change was obvious.

Super Bowl XIII was in the Orange Bowl in Miami against the Cowboys. Dallas had the Doomsday defense, and they were pretty good with Ed "Too Tall" Jones, Harvey Martin, and Randy White. They were No. 1 against the run that season. So, guess what? We planned to throw it.

In the week leading up to the game, Cowboys linebacker Thomas "Hollywood" Henderson caused a stir when he insulted the talent and intelligence of Terry Bradshaw. "Bradshaw couldn't spell 'cat' if you spotted him the 'c' and the 'a,'" he said.

Nothing was further from the truth. Terry was very smart, and we trusted him to call the right plays based on our game plan.

I guess it didn't matter if Terry could spell C-A-T anyway because he knew how to spell M-V-P. He was the most valuable player of the Super Bowl after passing for 318 yards and 4 touchdowns with just 1 interception. The Cowboys scored two late touchdowns to make the score look closer than the game really was, but we won 35–31.

It was one hell of an emotional moment for me.

You see, going into my freshman year of high school, they finally made my father retire from the railroad. My dad had to retire because he was now seventy-two years old. By this time, my mother was a self-taught anesthesiologist. The medical board came through with a regulation that you had to be certified. She wasn't.

I wanted to leave Mount Pleasant. We were talking about several places that were best for her to get employment. We decided on Rochester, Minnesota, because it was a great town, great people, and they had a great high school athletic program. It was everything I could hope for. We moved to Rochester to start my sophomore year of high school.

My father sat me down and told me he couldn't afford to send me to college after high school, and he was sorry. It wore on him, but that's the way it was. As I told you, my dad had it tough.

But in Rochester, with the athletic programs, I could find another way to college. I threw myself into sports. In three years in football, we went 26–1 and won a state championship. In basketball my senior year, I went to the state tournament, which was always on my bucket list. I always wanted to win a high school championship in football, which we did in Minnesota. The people in Rochester were fantastic. The school was great; the people were great.

We had been there about three or four months when my dad got up one morning and told my mother he wasn't going to sit there and wait to die. He wanted to get a job. So he went to Chicago to work for a guy who owned some racehorses. Make no mistake, he wasn't a trainer like Bob Baffert. For all practical purposes, he was a stableboy.

They had this one horse at Maywood Park named B'Haven. It was a big-time horse, but it was very high-strung. Now well into his seventies, my father took a cot and slept in the stall with the horse during electrical storms to calm it down. The owner of the horse didn't like that idea. My dad told him, "Well, I'll tell you what will calm that horse down. Buy a goat and you put it in the stable with the racehorse. It will calm his nerves." The owner bought a goat, and for whatever reason, it worked.

Because my dad worked in Chicago, he never got to see me play any high school games. My mother went to one football game, and we won 21–20, but she was getting up there in age. I came home and asked, "How did you like the game?"

She said, "That's it, I'm not going to any more games. My heart was beating too fast and all that stuff. I can't take it, Tom."

FUNNY STORY that became part of our Super Bowl XIV experience against the Rams at the Rose Bowl:

Back in those days, we didn't have Saturday afternoon meetings. We'd practice in the morning, and for home games, the team would meet at the Sheraton Hotel in South Hills Village, which was about two blocks from where Chuck lived. Chuck and the trainer would stay with the players, who had to check in by nine or ten o'clock. Curfew was at 11:00 p.m., but everybody went to bed because that's what you did.

Chuck told the coaches, "Take your wives out to dinner and spend some time with them." Then, Chuck and the trainer would stay back at the Sheraton, and we'd meet there Sunday mornings for the pre-game meal and go over any last-minute things. George Perles, Woody Widenhofer, Dick Walker, and myself would take our wives out to dinner, and we always made sure the first game we'd go out to someplace we liked because if we won, we'd have to go back for continued good luck.

In '79, before the season opener, we went to the Hong Kong Restaurant on Highway 19 in Dormont, Pennsylvania. So we won. So we went back. So we won again. So we went back. So we won. So we went back. Fortunately, they had good food.

The Chinese family who owned the restaurant believed they were the reason we won. Football coaches can be pretty superstitious, so we pretty much agreed.

We got to the point where the owner and the family finally invited us back into their personal kitchen to eat with them, which was a real honor.

So when we went to the Super Bowl in California, first staying at the Marriott in Newport Beach (a long way from the Rose Bowl), we were in for a pleasant surprise when the bus was just about to leave for a new hotel closer to Pasadena. George and Woody and I are coming out of the hotel, and here are these two Chinese men from the Hong Kong Restaurant with a bag of egg rolls. They paid their own way to California because they were afraid if we didn't eat their food before the game, we'd lose.

With our lucky food, the pass-coverage rule changes, and with Swann and Stallworth very proficient at reading defenses, we proved ourselves a passing team. Stallworth had a 73-yard TD reception and Swann had a 47-yarder.

I'll get into the plays that won our Super Bowls and how we came up with them later. But the Steelers had won four championships in six years. It was a dynasty for the '70s, and I'm grateful I got to be a part of it.

The Steelers were owned by a great family—the Rooneys—who still own the team today. I can't say enough good things about how they treated me and my family.

They would send the coaching staff anywhere we wanted to go after the Super Bowl. After Super Bowl XIII, we all got together and decided, "Let's go to Acapulco." All the coaches, their wives, Chuck and his wife, Dan Rooney and his wife. Well, that's eight couples. You can't do this kind of thing now with NFL coaching staffs. Christ, you'd have thirty couples.

We went deep-sea fishing one day and George Perles was down in the galley somewhere throwing up. So wouldn't you know it, I caught the fish. It was a giant marlin and I got two and a half hours of the finest coaching you'd ever want from Chuck while I brought in that fish.

He coached my ass off. He had to set the drag, all that stuff. The biggest thing I'd ever caught before was a two-pound catfish.

But George Perles was seasick and never got to witness this historic event. A guy from Minnesota catching a marlin off the coast of Acapulco.

After the '79 Super Bowl, our defense was starting to show their age. On the offensive side, Bradshaw had surgery to repair a torn ligament in his elbow after the '82 season when players went out on strike. He played only one game in '83, came to camp the next spring, and couldn't do it anymore—so he retired.

Bubby Brister started only one season at Division I-AA Northeast Louisiana (now the University of Louisiana at Monroe), but I took a liking to him at the NFL Combine in 1986. He was big and tough with a strong arm.

Brister remembered our first conversation: "Tom came and ate dinner with me at the combine and told me he liked the way I played and said, 'If I get a chance, I'm going to recommend that they draft you.' He gave me confidence that I would have success going and playing in that league."

In 1989, our Steelers team got blasted 51–0 by the Browns and 41–10 by the Bengals to start the season. We rebounded to finish 9–7 before upsetting Houston in overtime in the AFC wildcard game. The next week, we fell 24–23 in the divisional game at Denver.

Decades later, in the summer of 2023, Brister and running back Merril Hoge from that team attended my ceremony to receive the Award of Excellence from the Pro Football Hall of Fame. Brister told me he was crushed when I left the Steelers to join the Vikings as an assistant head coach.

"When you left, it hurt a lot," Brister said. "It set me back. We'd been together in the same system. It was a crusher." It's the first and maybe the only time I took another job for selfish reasons. There was no indication Chuck was going to retire. He still was relatively young and there just weren't any signs. You have a feeling about these things. The likelihood of me ever getting that head coaching job wasn't great, and I just kind of knew it.

I knew Vikings head coach Jerry Burns planned to retire in a couple years and I thought if I was on that staff, I would at least be considered for the Vikings head coaching job eventually. It didn't work out that way and that's okay.

PEOPLE WANT people on their side. Different people have different ways of expressing that caring. But Chuck was Chuck.

Chuck instilled a little bit of fear in his players. But I know he cared about them as athletes, as young men, as husbands, and as fathers. He cared about his coaches, too.

Chuck had one party a year. Just the coaches and their wives. It was always in April. We'd go to his house, and he did all the cooking. He would grill. He made all the drinks. He made sure the girls were happy. Then, when we got through eating, he'd sit in the living room and play his ukulele and all the girls would have sing-alongs. And Chuck was as happy as could be. You'd never know this was a Hall of Fame football coach. He loved to sing and then he'd get up and show us all how to do the Charleston.

At about one thirty in the morning, Chuck's wife, Marianne, would say, in a nice way, "I think it's time for you guys to leave." But we knew Chuck was staying up all night.

Some people think Chuck was a little bit shy. He wasn't going to go up and initiate conversation, but if you went up to him and started one, he'd talk forever. In my opinion, Chuck was reserved and selective.

And he loved to coach. *Loved* coaching.

In June of 1987, my wife and I spent five days with Chuck and Marianne. He had a forty-nine-foot Grand Banks boat. He'd park it different places and this year he had it in the Chesapeake in Oxford, Maryland. So we spent five days with him on the boat. He never mentioned football even one minute. One time I kind of started, and he said, "Tom, Tom, Tom. No football."

He could compartmentalize stuff. I'd see that with Peyton Manning, too.

God bless Marianne, she accepted Chuck's laser-beam focus. When it was time for football, nothing interfered with football.

5

From Bradshaw to Manning

TERRY BRADSHAW'S LAST GAME with the Steelers came in '83 against the Jets. It was the Jets' final game at Shea Stadium, and the New York fans acted as if it were the final sporting event of any kind there. After the game, they tore out the seats and went out on the field tearing up the sod. The Jets finished in last place in the AFC East that year, and although we'd fared better in terms of wins and losses, it had been a frustrating year for the Steelers quarterback.

Bradshaw went down with his elbow injury early in the season and Cliff Stoudt, his backup, had been playing. We got to our matchup with the Jets, the next-to-last game of the season, and we have to win it to make the playoffs after losing our three previous games. Bradshaw comes into my office Wednesday morning and looks at the game plan. He says, "Tom, do me a favor. Give me four runs and give me two play-action passes and two drop-back passes." So that's what we did. We had four runs, four passes. Sure, we could run them out of different formations, but we had just eight plays in the game plan. That was it.

Bradshaw threw 20 passes and we're up 20–0. He threw for 2 touchdowns in those 20 plays. On the 21st play, which was a pass, his elbow went and that was the end of Terry Bradshaw, quarterback. Last game. Last pass. I was right there to see it in Shea Stadium in New York.

We did win the game, 34–7, but after we dropped the last regular-season game to the Browns, the Raiders would beat us in Los Angeles to knock us out of the playoffs.

But that was an interesting finale to Terry's career. I remember Jack Lambert told an assistant coach before the game, "I see Bradshaw is going." Running backs coach Dick Hoak nodded. "He'll probably throw three touchdown passes," Lambert said.

And I'll be damned, but he nearly did.

I'm proud of Terry and all he's accomplished on and off the field. I was fortunate to coach him.

Eight plays in an entire game plan. If you had Franco Harris, Rocky Bleier, Lynn Swann, John Stallworth, and a healthy Terry Bradshaw, you might be able to pull it off. But other than Harris (who rushed for 103 yards and caught 2 passes for 13 more yards), all of them were injured or gone.

Some years later, Terry was already a big star in broadcasting when he called me after one of my games on the Colts' staff. He loved our offense and how much freedom Peyton Manning had at the line of scrimmage.

Bradshaw remembered the phone call, too: "I remember when Tom left Pittsburgh and, years later, he is coaching the Colts and Peyton is throwing for all those yards and I was so impressed. There Tom was on the sideline getting all the airtime. I was so proud of him. So proud. But also pissed! I called him and said,

'Excuse me. Excuse me for a second. But where the fuck was this offense when we were in Pittsburgh?'"

I'm 100 percent certain that Bradshaw could have handled the same offense. Hell, a lot of what we did with the Colts was similar to our Steelers offense.

The Steelers won the right to draft Terry Bradshaw by a coin flip with the Chicago Bears. Chuck Noll had gone 1–13 with the Steelers in his first season, tying Chicago for the worst record in the NFL.

Bradshaw was 6-foot-3 with big shoulders and a strong arm. But after his first four seasons, he'd been inconsistent with 41 touchdowns and 73 interceptions, including leading the league with 24 picks as a rookie. Still, by the time I arrived, he had won two Lombardi Trophies for Pittsburgh.

But as I mentioned, the Steelers were a team known for running the football and stopping opposing offenses with the Steel Curtain.

The Mel Blount Rule, prohibiting contact with receivers after five yards, arrived a year after me in 1978. Over the next two seasons, Swann and Stallworth combined to catch 213 passes and 33 touchdowns.

I hit it off with Bradshaw right away. Terry was everything you want in a quarterback. He was tough and smart. That's right, he was *very* smart.

That may go against Hollywood Henderson's assessment of Bradshaw's chances in a spelling bee, but

COACHING POINTS

MYTHS OF FOOTBALL

▶ *You Can't Win If You Turn the Ball Over.*

You can win, but it just makes it more difficult. I've seen coaches scare kids so bad, if they fumbled or threw interception, they thought the game was over. Keep playing.

it's true. Because of his southern roots and growing up in Shreveport, Louisiana, with that country accent, he didn't talk like everyone else. But an accent doesn't make someone stupid.

"I always tell everybody, when they're fussin' at me about the ol' I'm not very smart thing, I say, 'Oh yeah, I'm not very smart?'" Bradshaw said. "You believe that shit? Who called those plays? Who called all those plays? Who called those touchdowns? Who made all those adjustments? I'd have to defend myself, and Howie Long would say," 'You only had four plays.' I said, 'Yeah, but I had to decide, 'Do you run them to the right or do you run them to the left.'"

That self-deprecating sense of humor always served him well.

I was just a college coach from the University of Minnesota hired to coach receivers. But like Swann and Stallworth, Bradshaw welcomed me warmly.

"When Tom came over from Minnesota, I didn't know who he was," Bradshaw said. "I just loved the way Tom talked. I thought he talked really cool. He was such a positive guy and so freaking smart and a great listener. We would do stuff and I would say, 'Gol-lee, what if we change it to this?' And he would say, 'Yeah, we can do this or this.'

"He would've made a great offensive coordinator for us from the beginning. But back in those early days with Tom, we had five or six coaches, and everybody would meet and put a game plan together."

If Terry had any questions about the running game, he'd go to Dick Hoak, who knew it better than any coach I've ever known. If he had any questions about the passing game, he'd talk about it with me, Swann, Stallworth, and Jim Smith.

But Terry had a complicated relationship with Chuck Noll. He wanted a pat on the back once in a while, and that just wasn't Chuck. Some guys need it, guys like Terry.

"I respected Chuck Noll, but Chuck wanted me to be like Johnny Unitas," Bradshaw said. "He wanted me to be like Bob Griese. And I said, 'Well, Chuck, I don't know those guys. I don't know how to be like them.' What he was saying was, 'I want you to be more focused.' What he didn't realize is because you've got a personality and you're kind of goofy that it doesn't mean you're not focused. When I played, I wasn't in the huddle going, 'Hey, did you hear the one about the two drunks walking down the street?' No, no, no, no, no. I would've made a terrible captain. I didn't have time to do that shit.

"Tom was always in my corner, though. No matter what happened, he'd say, 'You keep throwing that sonofabitch.'"

I was the same way with Peyton Manning when I got to the Colts. I wanted him to be a gunslinger. I told him the touchdowns are yours, the interceptions are on me.

In his first season with the Colts, Peyton threw 28 interceptions, an NFL record (since broken when Jameis Winston threw 30 in 2019). There was some irony there: "I remember how many because he broke my record," Bradshaw said. Terry's count was 24.

But like Peyton, Bradshaw overcame all those interceptions his rookie year to win four Super Bowls and be inducted into the Pro Football Hall of Fame. It turns out, of all those Hall of Fame players and coaches on the Steelers, Terry is the most famous. He's won Emmys. He's done movies. He's a very successful businessman. He's also the only player I've coached who has a star on the Hollywood Walk of Fame.

"Yeah. But being the most famous doesn't have anything to do with being the most talented or gifted," Bradshaw says. "You've got to be a little versatile in life, I think. Another good thing about Tom, because I spent all my time with him, was the fact that he never tried to change me.

"I mean, I loved him. I would've loved to have played for him as my head coach, because I played better when I'm loved. My wife asked me this and I'll say, 'If I had played for Bum Phillips or someone who really loved up on me? I would've been so much better because I would've been free.' With Chuck, you were always on edge, which has its good points. I mean, obviously I can't complain. You get fucking tough with Chuck Noll. You've got to or you'll find your ass gone because he will push buttons. Tom Moore was just the opposite.

"But you know, it's like loving your child. It's called tough love. People respect that. People like me do, anyway."

That was just Chuck, and Terry Bradshaw will always be considered one of the greatest of all time. Of course, until Tom Brady won seven Super Bowls, it was Bradshaw on Mount Rushmore with four (before Joe Montana also won four with the 49ers).

Anyway, when the debate about who is the greatest quarterback of all time comes up, Terry is prepared in his patented head-scratching way.

"When they say, 'Tom Brady is the greatest who ever played,' I say, 'Really? Says who?' And they say, 'Well, he's won seven Super Bowls,'" Bradshaw said. "Yeah, he lost three. He played in ten and he lost three. Seven minus three is four. I played and won four. Montana played and won four and we lost none. That's math 101.

"I saw Roger Staubach in Dallas when Jimmy Johnson went into the Cowboys Ring of Honor. Staubach automatically started going back over the Super Bowls. I said, 'Roger, how old are you?' He said, 'Eighty-one.' I said, 'You got to let this go. You had a great career; I had a great career.'"

Terry Bradshaw laughed when I told him I wanted to title this book *Boots First* because that's how I'm leaving this world, hopefully on a football field during a game or practice.

"I've said the same thing at FOX," Bradshaw said. "I don't ever want to be fired; I just want to die right here. This is where I belong. This is where God blessed me to be, right here. And I said, 'Listen, if it does happen, look at the ratings!'"

"Spoken like a true TV guy."

WE'VE DISCUSSED BRADSHAW, and we met Bubby Brister. But the quarterback I'm probably most known for calling plays for arrived with an NFL pedigree and lots of pressure. I met Peyton Manning at the NFL Combine in 1998 and liked him instantly.

I had joined the Colts that year after leaving Pittsburgh and coaching in Minnesota, Detroit, and New Orleans. We had the No. 1 overall pick in the draft and general manager Bill Polian was making the selection. Would it be Peyton Manning from Tennessee or Ryan Leaf from Washington State?

We watched tape of both. Our Colts video team had every single pass Manning and Leaf had thrown collegiately.

At the NFL Scouting Combine, you got twenty minutes to interview each player in a room designated for your team at the Holiday Inn across from the old RCA Dome.

Peyton Manning walked in with a briefcase and a legal pad with two pages full of questions. He interviewed us!

I guess he didn't realize that if we drafted him, he had nowhere else to go. He was coming. But he had two pages of prepared notes, which is fine.

When Peyton got up to leave, he said, "If you draft me, I'm in town the day after the draft."

Bill told him that the rules dictated he couldn't come in until the week after the draft, but Peyton said he didn't care about that, he'd be there the next day.

Meanwhile, Ryan Leaf didn't meet with us at the combine. He stood us up. We were told later he was having an MRI, but that doesn't make any difference. He didn't come and he didn't tell us he wasn't coming.

Then we went to the private workout for Peyton. There was head coach Jim Mora; our quarterbacks coach Bruce Arians; myself; Dom Amile, our director of football operations; our receivers coach, Jay Norvell; scout Clyde Powers; and general manager Bill Polian.

The workout with Peyton Manning was excellent. His football smarts were off the chart. He had the whole thing scripted. He had his receivers and all the routes mapped out.

The knock against Peyton was that he had a ceiling on his arm. I would have him stand flat-footed and throw 20 yards. Then the guy who is catching it backs up 5 yards, so it's 25. He backs up another 5 yards. Thirty. Back up another 5 and it's 35.

You keep going and you see the arm strength, the velocity, the trajectory of the ball that he has to throw to get there. That's when Bill Polian made the statement that his ceiling was 60 yards just standing flat-footed. It's just coming up on your toes and throwing it.

"Okay," I told Bill. "We won't throw any passes more than 59 yards, how's that?"

Then we flew to Pullman, Washington, for Ryan Leaf's Pro Day. He could throw the damn football. Very strong arm. He was coming off a good Rose Bowl game, too, even though they lost to Michigan.

After the workout, Coach Mora went over to Ryan and asked him when he would be coming to Indianapolis if we drafted him. A week later, as the rules suggested?

He said he had planned a trip with some buddies to Las Vegas and he wouldn't be there. Mora asked about minicamp, and Ryan said he had a scuba trip planned in Cabo.

"We did one hundred tapes of them in the pocket, out of the pocket," Arians said. "Ryan threw it so well. Bill loved his arm, and it reminded him of Jim Kelly's. Peyton used to grunt when he threw it, like a tennis player. But we all agreed, Peyton is the guy."

The morning of the draft, Bill Polian came up to me and asked, "What would you do, Tom?" I said, "Well, Bill, a couple things. If you draft Ryan Leaf, you'll always wonder what it would've been like if you had drafted Peyton Manning. If you draft Peyton Manning, you couldn't care less."

Bill made the right choice and drafted Manning. And just like he said, he was in Indianapolis the next day. I met him at the old Signature Inn, we pulled the blinds shut in the hotel room in case anybody was watching, and I spent three days teaching him the offense.

We were a new staff. We hadn't practiced yet, so we really didn't have much tape to watch. What we'd do is meet a couple hours in the morning and a couple hours in the afternoon. We had a grease board, and we'd go over there and go through the playbook, go through all the terminology. We'd go through the plays that we were going to put in. The passing game. The reads and just the base foundation of the offense.

We had some film from stuff we had done previously when I was at Detroit, particularly. We copied a lot of that stuff that we did. But we probably spent four or five hours a day just going over stuff. Basically, it was terminology, reads, protections. That was a big thing. We spent a lot of time on protections. When I went into Indianapolis with Jim Mora, the cupboard was pretty bare. That's how you get the first overall pick in 1998 and get the third pick the next year, which we used to take running back Edgerrin James.

Peyton held out a couple days after camp started. He's in Indianapolis but he can't do anything. He missed a couple practices. We had Kelly Holcomb at quarterback. We finally got Peyton's signature on the dotted line, and we were in the middle of team work at practice. Bill Polian brought Peyton to the practice field. I looked at Holcomb, whistled, and shouted, "Kelly. Out."

In the meeting the next day, Holcomb gave us a laugh when he said, "You know, you guys need to be nice to me. You owe me a favor. If I hadn't played like horseshit against Minnesota the last game of the season, you wouldn't have been able to draft Peyton. So I'm the reason you got him, and you better be nice to me."

Jim Mora was our head coach, and he was really good. He was a great communicator. He had a lot of experience coaching the defensive side of the football.

He set the foundation and the groundwork. He was big on enforcing discipline, and it didn't bother him to do that. That was Jim. In other words, you're going to do things right and you're going to do what we tell you and it's going to be disciplined. He was good to work for. I'll say this, the whole time I called plays there, he never once second-guessed me.

And did Bill Polian ever question me? Not really. The only thing Bill ever said to me about play-calling was after the 2008 season and he was exactly right: we should try to get the ball to Dallas Clark more. The next year, Clark caught 100 passes for 1,106 yards and 10 touchdowns.

Our first year, we went 3–13. It's okay. We got Edgerrin James the next year from Miami and we got the ground game going.

Of course, it always starts with protection.

I've seen young quarterbacks get destroyed playing behind bad offensive lines and in schemes where they weren't protected. They get the crap knocked out of them and it destroys their confidence. So, Peyton's rookie year, we kept a lot of two tight ends in the game for that reason.

His rookie year was a struggle. Sometimes we didn't have that many receivers out and maybe nobody was open. Instead of Peyton throwing the ball away, he would try to throw it into some tight windows, and he threw what was then a rookie record number of interceptions.

Even though we went 3–13, you could see he was getting better, more comfortable as the year progressed. In Week 7, we got into a shootout at San Francisco against a very good 49ers team. We lost 34–31, but Peyton passed for 231 yards and 3 touchdowns with no interceptions.

The next year it really clicked. It helped that we were able to draft Edgerrin. Peyton figured out when to throw the football away and was making better decisions. A year after going 3–13, we went 13–3 and won the division.

I had answers. As a play-caller, the best thing you can do for a quarterback is have answers.

That's what Peyton Manning needed and demanded. That's what every quarterback wants and it's my job to come up with them.

When I was at Indy, we spread the field out with Marvin Harrison and Reggie Wayne, and we were going to run Edgerrin James outside until you stopped us. If you didn't stop it, we'd keep running it.

We played Green Bay once in Indianapolis; this was in 2004. I never scripted the first 15 plays. I had openers. Against the Packers, we threw on the opening play of the game. We wound up throwing 22 straight times. Twenty-two. The Packers defense opened the game playing their defensive backs at least 10 yards off the line of scrimmage, determined to stay in that soft zone to prevent the ball from going over their heads. More important, they kept blitzing so many men, it was tough to block them all to run the ball. So we kept our running back in to help pick up the blitz and I told Peyton to keep throwing it. My mindset was I don't care what you do, just give me the last call before the snap and we're going to try and beat whatever you are doing against the run or pass. After 22 straight passes, the score was 21–14. We'd score, Brett Favre would score, and it went back and forth. (We ended up winning the game 45–31, with Peyton throwing for 393 yards and 5 touchdowns, and Brett Favre throwing for 360 yards and 4 TDs.)

I told Peyton, "If they're doing that [playing their corners off the football], throw it every time." That's execution. That's what Peyton thrived on. Peyton thrived on being taught, and then being in control. And that's okay in my book. Yeah, I was the OC, but who gives a shit? Who cares who gets the credit?

Peyton has a great sense of humor, as everyone knows, and he liked to have a lot of fun off the field. But when it came to football, nothing interfered. At Indianapolis after Jim Mora's tenure, Tony Dungy used to allow all the players' and coaches' kids to come to Saturday practice. But Peyton didn't like that. To him, it was a distraction. There was nothing malicious about it. It's just how we did things. But in the end, Tony stopped allowing kids to come to Saturday practice.

Peyton also didn't wear a different-colored jersey at practice like other quarterbacks around the league. He wanted to be just one of the players. He said, "They know not to hit me." He may have worn one later on, but he didn't initially. When he came to Indy, his locker was right in the middle of the offensive line. He didn't want to be set apart. He just wanted to be one of the guys.

I think his father, Archie, taught him not only to embrace his offensive line, but also the entire community where he played. When you first came to Indy, you're the No. 1 pick, you go into town, and you buy a house. You're a resident. Everybody in that community knows that you live there. . . . Now, in the offseason, Peyton could live wherever he wanted to. But he bought a home in Indy, and the fans and the community loved him for it. Of course, everybody knows about his charitable donations. He's got a wing at Ascension St. Vincent's Children's Hospital.

Peyton was a role model. He was beloved. A lot of parents in Indianapolis named their sons and even their daughters after him. Because of that, he didn't face the kind of scrutiny that some other quarterbacks around the league did.

You know, a lot of people made a big deal about quarterback Russell Wilson having his own office in Denver with the Broncos. Peyton had one in Indianapolis. He got an assistant, too, a kid to handle all his non-football stuff, like the logistics of preparing thousands of autographed pictures. All Peyton had to worry about was football.

• • •

I'VE ALWAYS SAID THIS: it's about players, not the plays. We had a lot of smart players.

Continuity wins in the NFL. Even though Jim Mora was fired from the Colts after four seasons, I was able to stay as Tony Dungy's offensive coordinator and we kept rolling.

Tom Brady had Bill Belichick for twenty years in New England. Even though his offensive coordinators changed from Charlie Weiss to Josh McDaniels to Bill O'Brien and then McDaniels again, Brady was always in the same system.

It's not an accident that you have success with that kind of continuity.

And the most important thing you have to do is continuously protect the quarterback. Everything starts with protection The NFL is full of stories of teams taking quarterbacks high in the first round, but their inability to protect them has an immediate and sometimes long-lasting effect. David Carr was the first overall pick of the Texans in 2002, but he was sacked 76 times as a rookie. That was an NFL record at the time.

"I had great trust in Tom," Peyton said. "I liked him from the start, and he coached me and encouraged me during my rookie year, which was a struggle. We ran two receivers out in the pattern and maybe nobody was open and instead of throwing it away, I was still throwing it into tight windows and threw a lot of interceptions, but I wasn't getting hit a lot. I think that was his main goal. He'd seen quarterbacks come in and get the crap knocked out of them and they kind of lose their confidence and don't step into their throws and they never get it back. It was a plan that he was going to stick to, and we went from 3–13 my rookie year to 13–3 the next year because I kind of figured out when to throw it away and how to make better decisions. So I appreciate that approach.

"I felt like Tom always had answers for me, the plays that he called. I think as a quarterback, that's a great word to have. I have *answers*. He had a lot of sayings. It was always about players, not plays. He knew the things our players did well. He knew we had some smart players. He was very stubborn about some of the things he believed in. Whoever practiced the hardest played the hardest."

After a while, I would begin calling the play, and Peyton would cut me off at the beginning because he knew what I wanted. And I gave Peyton the authority to audible.

Chuck Noll told one of his quarterbacks, Bubby Brister, "Hey, you can audible, but it better work." That's not really trust, that's more of a threat.

"Tom called plays, but he gave me the freedom to audible," Peyton said. "He also gave me the freedom that if I pointed to my chest,

COACHING POINTS

THINGS YOU HAVE TO GUARD AGAINST

▶ *Death by Inches*

This is what gets teams. Super Bowl teams. A guy works out five times a week and after winning a Super Bowl, he says, "Maybe I'll work out four times a week." If he watched three hours of tape, he says, "Shit, I already know that." And he watches maybe an hour and a half and eventually it creeps into your habits and you die. Because the other guy in the other town, he's working out five days a week.

That's where Peyton was so good, and to me that's why Belichick was so good. It pisses a lot of people off. But it's like Nick Saban said, "If I wanted to be liked, I'd sell ice cream cones."

that meant, 'I got it.' He would wave and say, 'You got it.' He used to tell me, 'Hey, Payton, if you see something, you go with it. And if it doesn't work, I'll take the blame for it. I've got your back.'

"There was never a time I surprised Tom with a play call of mine or an audible because we'd talked about what we liked if the defense ever does this or that. You're in a situation where you're waiting for this team to play this one defense and they finally get to it in the third quarter and Tom is like, 'Hey, if you see it, let's get to that play because we may never see it again.' And that was a real advantage. He said, 'You have the best view of anybody out there.' I felt like I earned that trust and respect. That wasn't the case right away. It took me a few years to earn that. I wasn't going to call a gadget play. I called the plays we talked about that worked. I felt like we never surprised each other. But as far as the flexibility and answers, I never felt like we were stuck. Often, teams would come out and play something entirely different than they played the week before. You watch film, and with some teams it takes until after the game to figure out how to counter what they did. Our system, we had the answers. Tom had a huge call sheet and if they did this, you knew what to get to. That gives you a huge amount of confidence that we weren't going to be behind. We were going to have the answers."

I told all my quarterbacks to play smart, not scared. If it's there, take it deep, but don't feel like you have to force it. No guts, no blue chips.

Peyton took all the reps in practice. Every single one. He wanted to get a feel for the defensive looks he was going to get from our opponent. That's why it was important that our Colts defensive look squad, which simulated what we would see from the opponent on game day, gave Peyton and the offense the best picture possible.

If something wasn't quite right, if Peyton didn't like a certain play against a look the defense was giving us, we would talk about it on the practice field and fix it. My job was to give him answers to everything he and our Colts offense would see on game day.

One time, Jon Gruden was doing one of our games as a broadcaster on *Monday Night Football*. We got into the production meetings and he asked me, "Tom. I watched the whole practice and not one of your backup quarterbacks took a single rep. Why is that? Why does Peyton take every single rep?"

I looked at Jon and the other guys on the crew and said, "Fellas, if No. 18 goes down, we're fucked. And we don't practice fucked."

Here's a funny story, and our assistant equipment manager Mack Mays can back Peyton up on it. Smack was his nickname and he listened to the plays coming in on the helmet communicator in case something went wrong.

"My second year, Tom saw me and Marvin [Harrison] after practice working on a route in the red zone," Manning said. "It was kind of a post, slant, go, slant. Kind of a triple move, if you will. I told him we had been kind of working on it. Well, sure enough, we're playing the Patriots in Foxboro, it's our first drive, and we come out *bam, bam, bam*. We get down to about the 15-yard line, the area where Marvin and I had been working on this route.

"The NFL is supposed to be very sophisticated with all these complex terms and words. And Tom goes, 'Okay, here we go, Peyton. Let's go dice right, scat right—just run whatever the fuck you and Marvin were working on the other day.' Sure enough, we called it and we scored. He walked right up to us and said, 'See, it ain't that hard.' He's still that way today. Don't make it harder than it has to be. That kind of defines Tom in a lot of ways."

He's right. It isn't that hard sometimes. It's just not easy.

. . .

I HAD BEEN on the Steelers' coaching staff to see Bradshaw's last game. I was also a consultant with the Jets when Peyton Manning suffered a spinal injury in a game against the Redskins in 2011 that ended that year's campaign and caused him to miss the next season, as well.

The Colts went 2–14 without Manning, earning the No. 1 overall pick, which would become Stanford quarterback Andrew Luck.

Manning's resilience and determination fueled his incredible comeback. After his third neck surgery on September 8, 2011, he didn't attempt to throw a football until late December. That's when he made the first of several trips to Durham, North Carolina, to be reunited with his former Tennessee offensive coordinator, David Cutcliffe. For months, he worked out secretly with a few Duke players.

In March of 2012, Peyton invited me to go to his workout at Duke with Cutcliffe.

He called me up and said, "Tom, I want you to come to my workout just to see what you think." And he brought in center Jeff Saturday and Dallas Clark and I think Reggie Wayne, plus a couple of Duke receivers. Cutcliffe had a script and called the plays, and we worked with Peyton. After the workout, Cutcliffe asked me, "What do you think?"

I said, "If you didn't know, you wouldn't know. He looked good to me."

Peyton believed the Colts were hoping he would retire but he told me, "I ain't retiring." So they ended up cutting him and he went to Denver.

Little did we know that visit to Duke would be the start for both of us getting back to a Super Bowl: Peyton with the Broncos and me several years later with Bruce Arians with the Cardinals and the Bucs. Had it not been for my trip to Duke, I would not have met one of the nation's best orthopedists to fix my failing knees, which had kept me off the sidelines. I was in Phoenix coaching for Arians and the Arizona Cardinals after we lost to Carolina in the NFC Championship Game during the 2015 season. Watching Peyton Manning quarterback the Broncos to a 24–10 win over the Panthers in Super Bowl 50 was pretty emotional. I was thrilled for Peyton because of all he had gone through and all he had done for me and the Colts. He made me a better coach, and everyone in the Colts organization and the city is indebted to Peyton. If someone asked me to define what a professional athlete is, I would say, sit down and give me a few hours and let me tell you about Peyton Manning.

6

From Manning to Brady

I MET PEYTON MANNING before his NFL career even started. He would go on to win two Super Bowls and five NFL Most Valuable Player Awards. I got to know Tom Brady after he'd won six Super Bowls and three NFL MVP Awards. Quite a lot happened in the intervening years, and I'll cover that later. But I'd like to stick with these Hall of Famer quarterbacks I got to work with.

So, let's jump ahead to 2019. I'm with Tampa Bay as an offensive consultant. We were 7–7 following two amazing performances by quarterback Jameis Winston, who had just passed for 456 yards and 458 yards and 4 touchdowns in each game against the Colts and Lions to extend our winning streak to four.

The Texans and Falcons were up next. Both home games. So, a winning record was within our grasp. It looked as if Winston, who had struggled earlier in the season, had finally turned the corner.

But he threw 4 interceptions against the Texans, including one on his first pass attempt. Then he had 2 INTs in our loss to Atlanta in the season finale, including a pick six by linebacker Deion Jones in overtime. That gave Winston an NFL record 30 interceptions in one season. Somewhere Peyton Manning may have exhaled.

I walked off with head coach Bruce Arians after the game. He looked at me and said, "Well, that's it."

I knew we would have a new quarterback for the Bucs in 2020. I never imagined it would be Tom Brady, one of the greatest quarterbacks of all time, and our nemesis for all those years when I was with the Colts.

Tom was now forty-three years old. Peyton Manning had retired five years earlier after winning Super Bowl 50 with the Denver Broncos. They had become good friends. A mutual respect had grown from their many years as fierce competitors.

I think it was John Spytek, our vice president of player personnel, who coined the pursuit of Brady as Operation Shoeless Joe Jackson. Remember the movie *Field of Dreams*? The voice in the cornfield kept repeating, "If you build it, he will come."

Well, Jason Licht, Spytek, and the scouts had built a really good football team. We were a quarterback away. Few could believe that quarterback would be Brady.

What impact would Brady have on our Bucs team?

It was personified immediately when Chris Godwin stepped up and gave his jersey number to Tom.

Chris had worn No. 12 since high school. In fact, he was known as CG12. The gold necklace he wore said as much.

But immediately, Chris said, "That's Brady's number. I'll take 14." That set it off. That's how it started.

A lot of guys won't give up their number without being asked or compensated. In fact, Brady offered to take No. 10, which is what he wore at Michigan. But Chris wouldn't hear of it. That's how much respect everybody had for Tom Brady.

I know when I heard Brady was going to sign with us, I said out loud, "Wow. We're going to win this thing. We're going to win it."

Even at the ripe old age of forty-three, he was going to be the answer for the Buccaneers. I'd seen how Brady was playing. Most important, I knew what he brought to an organization: ownership.

Somewhere along the line, you've got to have a player who takes ownership the way that Brady did. He held everybody accountable. He took every practice rep seriously. He had high expectations for coaches and his teammates. Players had to match his energy and his effort. Immediately, you knew he was only about winning.

He came in and he made everybody better. He made coaches, the front office, the PR department . . . he made *everybody* better.

You see, we wanted to look good to Tom Brady. I mean, this is a two-way street. He came to what he thought was a first-class organization, and we knew we had better live up to that. He chose *us*.

I will never forget the first time he came through that door in my office. Bruce Arians; our quarterbacks coach, Clyde Christensen; and I had all viewed Brady as the enemy for so many years. Clyde had even joked that his grandkids might never speak to him again if he coached Brady.

But Tom Brady didn't just break the ice, he took a blowtorch to it. Brady could not have been nicer or more respectful. He shook my hand and said, "Hi, Coach." I said, "Hey, Tom.

Have a seat." There was a guy I coached with at Minnesota by the name of Dick Rehbein. He was a receivers coach for the Vikings but wound up at the Patriots as the quarterbacks coach under offensive coordinator Charlie Weiss. Dick is the guy that went to Michigan to assess their graduating quarterback. He didn't discover Brady, but he's the guy who pounded the table for Brady. He called me after that Michigan workout with Brady and said, "Tom, I just worked out the next great quarterback in the National Football League." I said, "Is that right?" He said, "It's Tom Brady. Trust me."

Belichick had told Dick, "We're going to draft a quarterback late," and to "go and find the best you can find."

Sadly, Dick never got to coach Brady. Dick had cardiomyopathy. He was on the heart transplant list when he was at Minnesota in the '80s and early '90s, and they took him off. He was doing a stress test at Massachusetts General in August 2001 when he passed way.

That first time Tom came in my office, I asked him, "Do you remember Dick Rehbein?" He said, "Yeah, he worked me out."

We talked a little about how strange it probably felt to be joining a bunch of former Colts coaches. It was pretty strange for us, too.

Then Tom went down and saw Bruce, who said, "I can't believe it. I just sat in the office with the guy I looked at on the other sideline and hated his guts and now I'm being friends with him."

It's hard not to like Brady, no matter how hard we competed against him with the Colts and Peyton Manning. There was always mutual respect.

It's nice to know that Tom liked me, too. He recalled "all the times, and there were a lot of them, that we would sit in the quarterback room and talk about so many of the amazing memories we had as competitors. And then once we're on the same team, you forget about all that. And all you do is have a great admiration and respect for one another. You know, we sat in quarterback meetings for three years together and I loved my time with him. He had amazing stories from when he coached the Steelers, all the way to the Colts and beyond. I just had tremendous respect for him."

Thinking back on those games, it's clear that Brady and Peyton made each other better.

Brady played Manning seventeen times, with the Patriots winning the head-to-head series 11–6. That included Manning's time with the Colts. They met five times in the NFL playoffs, with Manning winning three of them. The only constant was the home team always won. Five of those games were in the AFC Championship, and Manning took three of four.

"I always loved the Colts offenses," Brady said. "They were always so complementary in the run game, the pass game. They ran the stretch play and then they ran the stretch pass. They ran the power play, then they ran the power pass. And they were good in two-minute, they were good backed up, they were good on third down.

"I think Tom let Payton do a lot of things. There was a great ability for them to work together. From what Payton wanted, from what Tom wanted, and from what Clyde Christensen wanted. And they all worked together seamlessly to make things happen."

Peyton did all these things at the line of scrimmage, and by 2010, Brady was doing it, too. I don't know if the Patriots gave it to him, but he took it.

I gave Tony Dungy the same freedom at the University of Minnesota. The first year, I signaled in the plays to Tony. The second year, he shook me off like a baseball pitcher, and the third year, he turned his back to me.

Bradshaw called his own plays, too, and he was good at it.

Of course, Brady couldn't have picked a worse time to change teams after twenty years. COVID-19 had shut everything down in the spring of 2020. He couldn't meet with coaches. He went to get a playbook from our offensive coordinator, Byron Leftwich, and walked into the wrong house. Leftwich lived next door. He got kicked out of Tampa Park by the city's recreation department when he tried to work out there because it was officially closed. Eventually, Tom organized workouts at Berkeley Prep, a local high school.

Brady developed chemistry quickly but was still learning the offense on the way to the Mercedes-Benz Superdome the first game of the 2020 season. (We lost to the Saints in New Orleans, 34–23.) On his first drive, we took over at our own 15-yard line and we were in the end zone in 11 plays. Tom called his own number and snuck it across from the 2-yard line for a touchdown, spiking the ball high in the end zone as an exclamation point, the way Gronk would.

COACHING POINTS

MYTHS OF FOOTBALL

▶ **Field Position**
Whether it's bad or it's good, don't bitch about field position. Make a play and change it!

But that was about as good as we played all day. Brady went 23 of 36 for 239 yards and threw 2 touchdown passes. But he also was intercepted twice. One looked like a miscommunication with Mike Evans. The other was a pick six by Janoris Jenkins that gave New Orleans a 24–7 lead.

After the game, Bruce Arians didn't hold back when he was asked about how Brady played.

"He knew he didn't play very well," Bruce said. "It's not what he expects from himself, nor do we expect it. I would expect him to have a little more grit, a little more determination this week."

That's Bruce. Bruce has the "it" factor. Another coach might say what Bruce said, and the player would say, "Screw him!" I think Tom would've been disappointed if Bruce had done anything different. Bill Belichick called a spade a spade, too, you know.

Bruce felt we were a quarterback away from contending for a Super Bowl. Jameis Winston wasn't that quarterback. In his defense, he spent the time and he worked. But I think these guys saw a different level when Brady came to the Bucs with his work ethic and then the production.

We rebounded from that opening-day loss at New Orleans to start 6-2 before being crushed by the Saints at home, 38–3.

One thing that helped bring this team even closer together was the trip from hell, when we went to Carolina. We got stuck in Tampa. We were supposed to board our charter flight at two in the afternoon. The plane had mechanical issues, so we waited there for two hours. Then we taxied to the runway. We were there another hour. Then the airline announced, "This plane isn't going anywhere."

We had to get a new plane flown down from Atlanta. So we got in at ten thirty that night and got to the hotel about 11:15 p.m. All those night meetings and things we were supposed to have meant nothing. We had our pre-game meal at the hotel that morning and went out and won the game.

We didn't take the lead until early in the third quarter at 20–17. But backed up on our own 2-yard line, Ronald Jones broke off a 98-yard touchdown run, the longest from scrimmage in team history. Tom had a good game, throwing 3 touchdowns. We could all see him learning our playbook and personnel while incorporating more of the things he did in New England with protection and pre-snap motion.

It took some time, though. We were 7–5 after losing back-to-back games by 3 points to the Rams and Kansas City at home. Kansas City's Tyreek Hill had more than 200 yards receiving in the first quarter, on his way to a 269-yard, 3-touchdown day. Our defense had had some problems, but Todd Bowles learned some things about the Chiefs that would pay off later in the Super Bowl. One of the things that we changed more than anything else for Tom was the pass protection. A lot of our pass protections were slide protections where the running back had to read two people to get out. But Tom likes a protection where the line blocked the four bigs, plus the Mike linebacker, and the running back blocked the Sam or Will depending on which side you threw hot off of, and Brady felt comfortable with that. I'd say protection was No. 1 for him.

Remember, Tom arrived during the COVID-19 pandemic. There were no offseason workouts except the ones he arranged at a local high school. There were no preseason games. Even during the bye week, Tom wanted to get with Bruce Arians and spend some time together, but the protocols really didn't allow for it.

We didn't change much else; we just kept doing what we do and did it better. Defensive coordinator Todd Bowles did that on defense. Bowles didn't change and they got better.

No question the addition of Rob Gronkowski was key offensively because he was Brady's security blanket. When you watch

Gronk practice, he looks like a big, lumbering guy. Then, all of a sudden, he's wide open. I don't how he got so wide open because he looked like a big clod sometimes running, and then—whoop! He's open.

I think Gronk helped Tom to relax. He had his guy, on and off the field.

Gronk never had a bad day. He's the same guy you see on TV. He was always upbeat anytime you saw him. Tom is so intense. Gronk balanced Tom.

Gronk was the big, affable neighbor who always had your back. I lived in The Towers in downtown Tampa. I was on the fifth floor of one tower and Gronk was in the other tower. The dog park was right outside of my place. We're getting ready for a night game. I'm sitting there and I look out the balcony and here comes Gronk with his dog. It was a nice dog. It's four hours before we're supposed to kick off, and here's Gronk picking up dogshit before the game. He was smiling while he was doing it.

It's tough coming into a new team. But Brady and Gronkowski gave us the belief we could win it all.

The key was staying healthy and following all the COVID-19 protocols. Ryan Griffin, our third-string quarterback, said it best. He said he never went out to bars or restaurants during the pandemic because he didn't want to be the guy to give Tom Brady COVID.

He had an impact on the whole team. He had an impact on me, too.

If I saw little things he could correct or take advantage of, I would tell him. When he first came, I told him, "I watch, I observe, but I don't talk a lot, Tom. But I see something, I'll tell you." Clyde Christensen was his quarterbacks coach, and I didn't want to interfere.

He said, "Hey, Coach, any way you can help me, please do." That's who he was.

WE ALWAYS FELT like we were going to win the game. Brady didn't win them all single-handedly. But we always felt like we were going to win because we had Tom Brady.

It didn't matter how much we trailed in the fourth quarter. We knew we had a chance. He proved it with the Patriots when he came back from being down 28–3 to beat Atlanta in Super Bowl LI. It was the same thing with Peyton. We were down 18 points in the AFC Championship Game against the Patriots in January 2007 when we beat them to go to Super Bowl XLI. When you get those two guys playing, I know the Patriots felt like they were going to win it and we did, too.

Even when our Bucs team was a mediocre 7–5, I felt like we were going to win Super Bowl LV. I mean, we weren't even close to rolling through that season. Twelve games in, and we were fighting for our lives. But we got hot at the right time. Brady began to trust his protection. Gronk continued to make plays and Antonio Brown changed the whole dynamic of the passing game as a third receiver who could stretch the defense.

That's what it takes to win a championship.

After we fought our way to the playoffs, I figured there was no question we'd beat the Redskins in the first round. But they had a young quarterback, Taylor Heinicke, who stepped in for an injured Alex Smith and played his tail off, throwing for 306 yards and a touchdown while rushing for another score. We escaped with a 31–23 win. After that, I didn't know how we'd beat the Saints in the divisional round but I knew we'd find a way. We trailed by a touchdown late in the third quarter when Antoine Winfield Jr. forced a fumble by Saints tight end Jared Cook that Devin White picked up and returned to the Saints 40. That's all we needed.

Brady tied the game with a touchdown pass to Leonard Fournette and our defense took over the game. White had an INT and Tom ran one in.

We got out of the Superdome with a win.

The next week in the NFC Championship Game at Green Bay, the touchdown to Scotty Miller right before halftime was the main difference, giving us a 21–10 lead.

Our defense was terrific against Aaron Rodgers in the big moments. He was the MVP of the league and played like it, throwing for 346 yards, but we were strong when it mattered most. Brady had a rough second half with 3 interceptions. Still, he did enough in the fourth quarter to help us run out the clock.

Unlike the season opener at New Orleans when he called out Brady for missing some throws, this time Bruce Arians had nothing but hugs for his quarterback.

We won three playoff games on the road to reach the Super Bowl, becoming the first team to play that game in their home stadium. But that's one of those myths I don't believe in, that you can't win three road playoff games to get to the Super Bowl. Pittsburgh did it in 2005 as a wildcard team.

There was no doubt within the organization that we would beat Kansas City in Super Bowl LV. Everything was set up perfectly for us. We were healthy, our defense was playing great and getting turnovers, and Tom was as locked in as he had been in any game that season. He threw 3 touchdown passes: two to his buddy Gronk, and another to Antonio Brown. Both had come to Tampa Bay to play with Tom.

After we won the Super Bowl, we had a boat parade down the Hillsborough River. There's never been a celebration like that for a Super Bowl champion before or since and I'd been part of three of them to that point. COVID was still a big concern, but the event was outdoors, and the Bucs fans lined both sides of the river.

Tampa has a beautiful waterway through the city that leads to the Gulf of Mexico. The sun shined brightly, and you could feel the added warmth from the fans.

Tom later blamed it on too much avocado tequila, but for some reason he decided to toss the Lombardi Trophy from his forty-foot boat, *Viva a Vida*, to one carrying a bunch of our receivers and tight end Cameron Brate. Fortunately, like most of Tom's passes, this one was complete. Brate caught the trophy by the sterling silver football. Like I told our GM, Jason Licht, in practice, "You know, even when he throws a bad pass, you've got a chance to catch it."

Tom caught a lot of heat for that, but probably not as much as Gronk caught in New England when he dented the Lombardi Trophy while swinging it like a baseball bat.

Anyway, that was some kind of parade.

We wanted to defend our Super Bowl title. Bruce Arians got on the podium after the boat parade and said, "We're going to go for two!"

I thought Jason Licht did a great job of finding a way to re-sign all our free agents and we returned twenty-two starters to our 2021 team, including Brady.

But it's hard to win one Super Bowl, much less two in a row.

• • •

By the time we got to training camp the next year, Peyton Manning was being inducted into the Pro Football Hall of Fame. Tom had grown very close to Peyton through the years. We had a day off from camp, and more than anything else, Tom wanted to make sure Peyton's old Colts coaches got to be at the induction ceremony. So he very generously chartered a private jet to Canton, Ohio, and invited Bruce Arians, Clyde Christensen, and me to come with him so we could see Peyton become one of the NFL's immortals.

The network cameras were all aimed at Brady when he entered the stadium in Canton for the Pro Football Hall of Fame induction ceremony. He was led backstage, where he and Manning greeted each other.

It was a great time for both quarterbacks. Manning was minutes away from unveiling his bust. Brady, finally out from under the COVID-19 protocols, was able to support his rival and receive congratulations for winning his seventh Super Bowl ring.

Manning began by saying he felt like he needed to run the hurry-up on his speech, which had been limited to six minutes for the first time ever because, prior to that, some would run more than a half hour.

Manning also acknowledged Brady in the audience: "And speaking of rivals, my good friend Tom Brady is here tonight. By the time Tom Brady is inducted in his first year of eligibility in the year 2035, he'll only have time to post his acceptance speech on his Instagram account."

Meanwhile, Brady had a big date circled on his calendar, his first trip back to Foxboro to play the New England Patriots on October 3.

For Brady to return to Gillette Stadium in front of those fans was going to be a special night. Tom got an enormous ovation when he came out for warm-ups but then once the game started, the Patriots fans were rooting like hell for their team, and he was playing like hell to beat them.

When Tom left the Patriots, there was a debate about whether those New England Super Bowls were fueled more by the genius of Tom Brady or by Bill Belichick. I don't know if that debate completely drove him, but the fact that he won a Super Bowl without Belichick made him feel very good, for sure. He got to see there was another way to win.

Maybe he just wanted a change. Maybe he just wanted to see what it was like somewhere else. Because they always planned to honor him when he went back to New England, and obviously, the brass at New England were in touch with Tom. Whatever went on, time tends to heal, and it looks like it healed in this case.

It rained the whole game. It was a hard-fought, back-and-forth affair. Rookie Mac Jones played well for the Patriots, going 31 of 40 for 275 yards and 2 touchdowns. But Brady engineered one of his patented fourth-quarter drives. He got us into field goal range late in the game and Ryan Succop kicked the game-winner.

New England had one final chance to win, but Nick Folk's 56-yard field goal try hit the left upright and was no good. After the game, Tom and Belichick embraced at midfield. And later in our locker room, Belichick and Patriots owner Bob Kraft came over to Tom's locker and they all talked for about twenty minutes.

It was highly unusual. But now 1–3, it told me at that particular time, the Patriots were missing him a little bit more than they thought they would.

Whatever there was between them, it was over by the time Tom left Foxborough that night. People who watched the meeting between Brady and Belichick said it was very cordial. Brady called it "a very private, personal thing." He has always denied reports that he and Belichick's relationship had been fractured in the later years.

I sat in on all the meetings leading up to the game and I never heard Tom say one negative thing about the Patriots. We all knew it meant a lot to win that game for Tom. I felt that. The other coaches did, and I think the players did. Let's win this one for Tom. He tried to downplay it, of course. But we knew what it meant, and justifiably so.

We won the NFC South and won our first wildcard playoff game against the Eagles at home. We fell behind the Rams the next week and trailed 27–3 in the third quarter. But remember, when you have Tom Brady, you always have a chance.

Our defense got us a couple turnovers and Tom brought us back. When Leonard Fournette scored a touchdown on a 9-yard run with 42 seconds left in regulation and Ryan Succop made the extra point to tie the game, I thought it was ours. There was no question in my mind. We had the momentum. Everything.

But we left too much time on the clock. Forty-two seconds would be enough for Matthew Stafford to send the Rams to the NFC Championship Game.

It started well. On the first play, Ndamukong Suh sacked Stafford, forcing the Rams to burn their final time-out with 35 seconds left.

Stafford hit Cooper Kupp on a crossing route for a first down. Then Todd called Cover Zero. He was coming after Matthew Stafford. That's what we had done all year. Stayed aggressive. You do what you do. Don't second-guess. As I say, 90 percent of calling plays is execution. And you can't play scared. Play smart, but don't play scared. We played smart.

Stafford connected with Kupp on a 44-yard deep ball and that set up the game-winning field goal by Matt Gay, who we had cut after his rookie season in 2019.

Our season was over.

For a while, it looked as if Tom Brady's NFL career had come to an end as well, but he wasn't prepared to make any announcements after the game.

The 49ers would've been coming to Tampa for the NFC Championship Game had we won. It would've been Tom Brady against Jimmy Garoppolo, and we wouldn't have lost that one.

There was a lot of speculation about Tom's future. He was forty-four years old, but I thought he had an MVP season. He led the NFL with 5,316 passing yards and 43 touchdowns.

He could still play, no question.

A few weeks passed and Tom announced he was retiring. We had to proceed as if he wouldn't be back. We were looking at free agents, such as Baker Mayfield, and Bruce was preparing to have Kyle Trask and Blaine Gabbert shoot it out in the training camp for the starting job.

But then forty days after he walked away, Tom announced he was coming back for "unfinished business."

I got a kick out of Bill Chappell, a writer for NPR News, saying that Tom Brady didn't retire, he just gave up football for Lent. Being an old Catholic, I thought that was funny.

But that's just Tom. He's got to have it and he thinks he can still do it. You go through a period of time in your life and think, "Why should I give up something I love that I can still do?" That would be like me giving up coaching.

I thought in my mind that he would come back, personally. I didn't know it would be quite as dramatic, but that comes with being a superstar. He came back, and things started to unravel.

Shortly after Tom announced he was ending his retirement, Bruce Arians announced he was stepping aside to let Todd Bowles become the head coach while Bruce took a position of senior assistant to general manager Jason Licht.

I think it was hard for Bruce to walk away, but I also think the way things ended in Arizona weighed on his mind. When he left there, for whatever reason, he thought that one of his guys would get the job and that the other guys would be taken care of. I think it hurt him when that didn't happen because he was loyal to the death. When this came up, when he had assurance that one of his guys would be named head coach and his assistants were all going to be taken care of, he felt it was time. He'd won a Super Bowl.

I also think Bruce was concerned about his health. He had to go to the hospital during the season for what turned out to be pericarditis. If it happens one time, what makes you think it won't happen again? And he'd had some health problems before. He was coaching practice out of a golf cart, which wasn't a hell of a lot of fun.

When Tom announced he was ending his retirement to return to the Bucs, Bruce saw an opportunity to get what he wanted. He knew he could win a Super Bowl as a head coach. He'd done it. Would he like to win two? Sure. But there's also your health factor and the staff factor. He could take care of all those things.

With Brady coming back, he could leave Todd with a real chance to win instead of leaving him with a team that was starting over.

I saw Bruce three weeks after he retired and he looked twenty years younger, refreshed. To this day, he's enjoying his grandkids and he's a good golfer. It's the best of all worlds. Everything is timing and it's right.

WE STARTED TRAINING CAMP in 2022, and on the second day, there were some ominous signs.

Our center, Ryan Jensen, had rookie defensive end Logan Hall fall across his left knee during a non-contact, two-minute period while he was engaged with defensive tackle Vita Vea.

Nobody will forget the sound of the scream Jensen made when it happened. You knew it was bad. He tore his ACL, MCL, PCL, and some cartilage. Season over.

The next day, Tom wasn't at practice. Todd told the media he had an excused absence.

What we know now is that his wife, Giselle, had filed for divorce. That's tough, and I'd been through it with Scott Mitchell, our quarterback in Detroit. He got served some time during the first week of training camp. He'd just come off a good season, and going through a divorce devastated him.

This job is hard enough. That's why I say when it comes to your career in football and family sacrifice, it's 80–20. It was hard on Tom. He had a lot to worry about off the field. Two of his kids, Vivi and Ben, were now with him only half the time. His oldest son, Jack, still lived in New York. Then you throw in the money that he lost in cryptocurrency.

To me, Tom did a fantastic job of functioning at all. A lot of guys would be knocked to the ground. You'd have to be a Tom Brady–type guy to do what he did that year. All of a sudden, you're going home to an empty house. Every day you pick up

Here I am, age 17, at basketball practice.

(*right*) Same age, in my Rochester High School football uniform in Minnesota.

(*below*) Iowa freshman team. Coach Jerry Hilgenberg, Bernie Wyatt, me, unknown, Bill Ringer, Don Zinn, Robert Mosley, and Tony Russo (left to right)

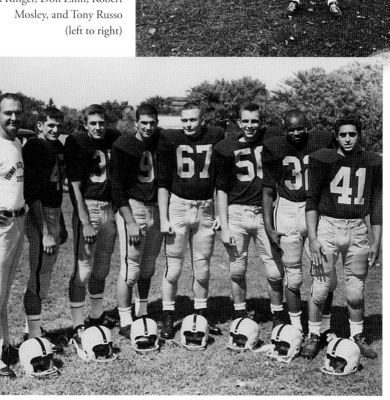

(*left*) Yours truly with my flat top in Korea.

(*bottom*) Coaches of the Korea Football team in the Army. Isiah Brown, Dwayne Klevin, me, Mike Steinmetz, and Sgt. Aki (left to right)

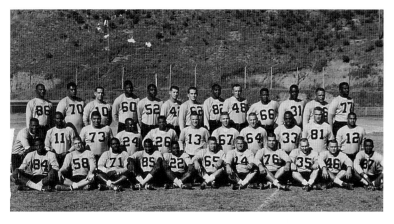

US Army football team in Ft. Benning.

Ft. Benning coaching staff: Mickey Heineken, me, Colonel George Peterson, Ken Schroeck, Don Harnum (left to right).

At Ft. Benning, Bill Williamson (All American at Georgia Tech) and Pat Dye, football team members with me—the coach—in the middle.

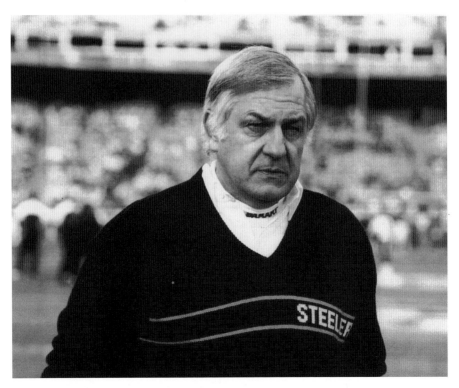

During my time as a receivers coach with the Pittsburgh Steelers.

I'm the coach on the right here, when I was a receivers coach with the Pittsburgh Steelers.

Tony Dungy, Colts offensive line Coach Howard Mudd, quarterback Peyton Manning, and me at the 101 Club in Kansas City when Manning was named the American Football Conference (AFC) MVP by the club, 2007.

When I was offensive coordinator with the Colts in 2006.

Here with quarterback Peyton Manning during our time with the Colts in 2008.

Mel Blount, Tony Dungy, and me at Blount's celebrity dinner, 2011.

Cardinals Head Coach Bruce Arians and me, when I was the senior offensive assistant in 2017.

Coaching with Cardinals quarterback Carson Palmer in 2017.

Posing next to the Vince Lombardi Trophy with the Bucs.

My headshot with the Tampa Bay Buccaneers in 2019.

(*below*) Yours truly, Bucs quarterback Coach Clyde Christensen and quarterback Tom Brady, former Colts and Broncos quarterback Peyton Manning, and Bucs Head Coach Bruce Arians before a Tampa Bay game at Denver, 2020 (left to right).

60 Prevent, Slot Hook & Go: This was a key play the Steelers used twice in Super Bowl XIV. John Stallworth was the slot receiver. It went for a touchdown from Terry Bradshaw to John Stallworth, which was one of the iconic plays in this game. It also resulted in another a 65-yard pass that set up a Franco Harris touchdown run.

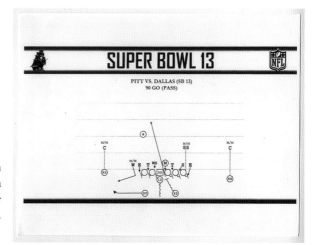

93 Tackle Trap: A run to Franco Harris for a touchdown in the Super Bowl XIII.

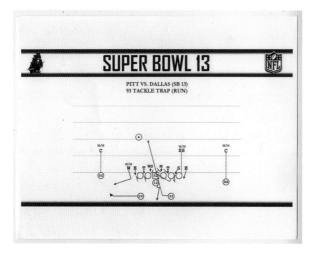

90 Go: A pass play to Franco Harris to counter a double A-gap blitz that went for 25 yards in Super Bowl XIII against Dallas. Another "answer" that the Steelers and I devised to counter their defense.

the paper and they're writing about you and Gisele. You might not read it, but you know the whole world is reading it. It was tough.

I was very worried about him. He was losing weight. I think he lost about twenty pounds. His face was drawn. And injuries were more likely at that time because there was more on his mind—yes, even on the field—besides football. You may pause, you may not be quick enough in your movement. What happens if he takes a shot? Truly, I'm surprised that didn't happen. You're out there and that's a dangerous place on that football field. You can't lose any concentration or you're going to get it. But Tom got through it.

The combination of events affected the entire team. The injury situation, starting with Ryan Jensen. There wasn't that cohesiveness that you'd had previously. If it affects Tom, then it affects the guy next to him, and all of a sudden, it affects everyone.

Tom was also really missing Gronk, who had retired (again) after the 2021 season. That man was his security blanket, on and off the field.

Yes, football is a tough business, and even tougher when you have family strife. There wasn't anywhere Tom could really be happy and where things were going well. I know he confided a lot with Byron Leftwich, our offensive coordinator.

Somehow, we started 2–0. For the second year in a row, we upset the Cowboys. This time, in Dallas, 19–3. Our defense played great, and we ran the ball well.

The next week we beat the Saints 20–10. Again, the defense played great, and didn't give up a touchdown until the fourth quarter. But we didn't score a touchdown until the fourth quarter, either.

We were 2–0, but we weren't exactly playing great on offense. Pretty soon, the wheels came off.

We lost five of our next six games. The low point came in a span of four days. We fell at Carolina 21–3, failing to score a touchdown. Then, four days later, we fell behind the Baltimore Ravens and lost 27–22 to drop to 3–5. Remember, Brady had never had a losing season in his career. He took it hard. Everything was coming to a head.

We didn't know it at the time, but the next day his divorce would be announced in a joint statement. Brady sat facing his locker in full uniform with his head between his legs for about twenty minutes after the Ravens game. He didn't move. He didn't acknowledge anything being said to him by Blaine Gabbert, our backup quarterback, who tried to console him.

From there, Brady started to build himself back up. We started playing better. You can bluff yourself and fool yourself into thinking personal matters aren't affecting you on the field. You want to get to the Super Bowl, but man, you know you'll be glad when the Super Bowl is over. It wore on the guy. You don't know what to say. One time I told Tom, "I don't mean to butt into your personal business, but I'm here to help you." He and Byron had a pretty close relationship. Both were quarterbacks in the NFL, competed against each other, and understood the pressure of that job on and off the field. I know he leaned mostly on Byron and Clyde.

He didn't have the year he wanted. But in my eyes, he was one of the greatest quarterbacks to ever play in the National Football League.

Look, everybody has problems. Every team has problems. And the team that handles the problems the best wins. If you go off half-cocked and half-crazy, you don't win. But a team that logically sits down and tries not to create more problems, that's the team that wins.

When you do win, you have to get hot at the right time and everything has to click. You've got to hit it just right.

We managed to win 8 games and the division. We clinched it with a win over Carolina at home the next-to-the-last week of the regular season. We trailed in that game 14–0 and 21–10. But Brady, as he has always done, put the team on his shoulders. He had his best game of the season, passing for 432 yards and 3 touchdowns to Mike Evans, who kept running behind the Carolina defense. Tom scored the winning touchdown with a quarterback sneak, spiking the ball like his buddy Gronk.

We only let him Tom play a few plays the next week at Atlanta as we rested many of our starters and lost to finish 8–9. We hosted the Cowboys in the wildcard game, but this time they beat us 31–14 in a game that wasn't that close. Tom's parents were waiting for him in the tunnel as we walked off the field. For all that he had been through, he had every reason to hold his head high.

One year to the day after he announced his first retirement, he retired again. This time, I had a feeling it was for good.

7

The Quarterback
I've Known the Longest

TOM BRADY WAS WITH US only three seasons in Tampa Bay and helped put Super Bowl rings on our fingers. But the quarterback I've known the longest is Tony Dungy, who would wind up being my coaching colleague with the Steelers and the Vikings, and then my boss as head coach of the Colts.

The first time I saw Tony Dungy, he was an excitable eighteen-year-old guard for the Parkside High School basketball team in Jackson, Michigan. He also was a quarterback who Woody Widenhofer and I had been recruiting to the University of Minnesota, despite knowing he'd always dreamed of playing for Duffy Daugherty at Michigan State, which was about twenty-five minutes away in East Lansing. Our ace in the hole at the time was that Minnesota agreed to let him play both sports in college—basketball and football.

Sherman Lewis, who played halfback for the Spartans, was now a member of Michigan State's coaching staff. He was at the same game to recruit Tony. As fate would have it, years later, Lewis would receive the Award of Excellence from the Pro Football Hall of Fame with me.

It was Woody and me versus Sherm at a Friday night basketball game. But not just in a contest to best evaluate Tony in the heat of battle or to woo him postgame. We were there to score points with Tony's parents.

Both of Tony's parents were impressive. His father, Wilbur, had a PhD in physiology, which he taught at Jackson Community College. His mom, Cleomae, was a schoolteacher at Jackson High School, which was Parkside's biggest rival.

Anyway, Lewis decided to sit next to Wilbur that night, and I made the wise decision to sit with Cleomae. Lewis had the home state advantage, but Wilbur didn't say very much. I always tease Sherm about his choice to sit next to Tony's father, while my strategy was to sit next to his mother, who talked the whole night.

"That's exactly what happened," Dungy said. "My dad was a big fan and all that, and so everybody kind of gravitated toward him. But my mom was the driving force, and she was very outgoing and her and Tom developed a relationship.

"During that time, Woody Hayes called our house once a week. He never talked to me. He talked to my mom. We were getting close to making a decision and my mom says, 'You know, you really ought to think about Ohio State.' Now, I'm in Michigan and everybody in Michigan hates Ohio State. But my mom says, 'Oh, he's such a great guy' and 'he's this and that. You ought to take a look. You ought to take a visit.'

"But Tom and my mom developed a relationship. They talked, and we decided I should take a visit to Minnesota."

The problem was Tony had never flown on a plane before.

"So I'm getting nervous, and I don't know if I can do this," Dungy said. "And I called Tom and I said, 'I don't know about this.' And Tom said, 'I'll come get you,' and he came and flew with me. Otherwise, I don't think I would have gotten on the plane.

"From a recruiting standpoint, he said, 'You can be great. You can define this offense.' But it was none of the hype you would get from everybody else," Dungy said. "It was, 'You've got to work on this. You got to do that. You got to be better here.' But he was a straight shooter."

Tony had some adjusting to do. We signed him and arranged for him, as soon as he graduated from high school, to come to Minneapolis so he and I could meet. We were going to get him a job. He could work during the day and make a little money. And when he got through with work, he could walk to the facility and he and I could meet.

He came to me after about two weeks and said, "Tom, you've got to get me a new job." I said, "Oh, yeah? What's the matter with it?" Well, I got him a job in a meatpacking place called Feinberg's. He was on a conveyor line where they had to stuff this sausage. He said, "I woke up last night and I was having a nightmare that I got behind on the conveyor belt and the sausage was wrapping around my neck and strangling me." He said, "The problem is I walk to this meatpacking plant and then I walk to the facility." He smelled so strongly of the meat that stray dogs would start following him. He said, "You've got to get me another job."

Dungy laughs when he hears this story. "I couldn't figure it out," he said. "I told him, 'Next year, I'll get my own job.'"

"But after work, I'd come to the facility at about four thirty. He would be there, and we'd work out. We'd be on the grease board at that time. I didn't know he'd been there since three in the morning. My time started at four thirty in the afternoon and we had some good times. I learned a lot of football.

"We hit it off. Tom was a lot like my dad in that very businesslike, straightforward, no-frills, no-BS demeanor. I was used to dealing with that and I loved it. He coached all of us hard, but he prepared you. I loved the work. I loved the learning, and he taught you the game and it was great."

Early on, I noticed Tony had a bit of a problem controlling his anger. He was very intense. That might sound hard to believe when you see how he has been as a coach, with his quiet, authoritative leadership style.

I told him, "If you're going to be the quarterback for this team, then you've got to be under control."

Tony had heard that before in Jackson. "My dad had been telling me that for years, but I didn't listen to my dad," Dungy said. "But now when my coach says you're not going to play until you get under control, I had to learn how to do it and it helped me the rest of my career. It was getting technical fouls in high school, getting into fights. I got thrown out of games. He liked the competitive part of it, but I can't lose control. I can't be off the rails even though I get upset, so you've got to learn how to control this, and I did eventually."

Before Tony Dungy arrived at the University of Minnesota, Woody Widenhofer took a job with the Steelers. I would meet with Tony in the afternoons during the summer. But once the season started, he would beat me to the office sometimes and have to stand outside in the freezing air. "I'd be there early waiting for Tom, and he said, 'We can't have this,'" Dungy said. "So he got head coach Cal Stoll to get me a key so I could go inside. I loved to work. I loved to learn, and he loved to teach, and it was awesome."

Yeah, things really clicked with Tony. When I left for the World Football League for one year and came back, I was given a larger role.

"Coach Stoll put Tom in charge," Dungy said. "He was the quarterback coach first, then he came back and put the offense in, so now we had a pro-style offense, and it was exactly what we were doing in Pittsburgh a few years later. The quarterback controlled everything. It was no huddle. I looked at him and he would give me a couple plays. We had to just kind of get on the same page, so we knew what we were looking at."

Tony Dungy was a great college quarterback and he thought he would be drafted. He wasn't. Several teams wanted to sign him, but none wanted him behind the center. The Bills wanted to sign him as a free safety. A number of other NFL teams called him offering a $1,000 or $1,500 bonus.

By 1977, there had only been six Black quarterbacks who had started games in the NFL: the Broncos' Marlin Briscoe; James Harris, who played for the Bills, Rams, and Chargers; the Steelers' Joe Gilliam; the Jets' J. J. Jones; the Bucs' Parnell Dickerson; and the Browns' Dave Mays.

It wasn't unusual as a Black quarterback in college to be drafted for your athleticism with the understanding you could help the team at another position besides quarterback.

Dungy's most lucrative offer came from Montreal of the Canadian Football League, where Bill Polian was the general manager. They wanted to pay Dungy $50,000.

Back in those days, the NFL Draft lasted two days. Toward the end of the draft, teams sent coaches like me to big cities to go get undrafted free agents. The Steelers sent me to Minnesota after I talked them into believing Tony wouldn't get drafted. When he doesn't get the call, I'd sign him. I told Tony I was in town, and if the draft passed him by, not to worry.

Well, he didn't get drafted.

I met with him and told him what the offer was. The Steelers told me I could go to a $5,000 signing bonus but to start negotiations at $2,000. I decided I'm starting at $5,000 because I don't ever want anyone to think I cheated them. While I'm going through my spiel, Tony tells me, "Hey, Tom, Buffalo is talking to me." I don't have a lot of tact and diplomacy sometimes. I said, "Tony, you ain't going to Buffalo. You're going to Pittsburgh, man. I don't give a shit what they offered you. You're going to Pittsburgh because it's the best place for you." His contract with the Steelers was $15,000; $17,500; and $20,000.

We had Bud Carson as our Steelers' defensive coordinator. Bud was a great defensive coordinator. Not a good one. A great one. But you had to know how to handle Bud. You couldn't jam things down his throat. I couldn't walk into Bud's office and say, "Bud, this is Tony Dungy. He played quarterback at Minnesota. He's your safety now." It didn't work like that. Instead, I told Chuck, "Here's the deal. I'm coaching receivers. Let's make a receiver out of him. He can run fast and he can catch." And Chuck said, "Good idea."

I told Tony, "You may be a defensive back eventually, but we've got to orchestrate this for you." He came and played receiver, and he got lots and lots of reps.

The rookies and the guys on IR, they came in a week early and then the veterans came in for two weeks. I also told Tony he would get lots of snaps in the preseason games because we don't play the vets much in those matchups.

Now, camps in those days were two full sessions in pads every day. And Bud was running thin on safeties. That was my chance. I said, "Hey, Bud. Tony is doing a pretty good job for me at receiver. He'll make the team. But he's not going to play a lot. If you can use him, if it can help you at safety, he's a smart guy and he knows his shit."

I'd caught Bud at the right time. "Good idea," was all he said. So Bud took Tony and Bud wouldn't give him back. Tony was so smart; it wasn't long before he could line other people up. He was like a quarterback on defense back there. It's no surprise. He had been a quarterback his whole life. "Tom knew my whole background was offense, but they always thought safety was the spot," Dungy said. "He said, 'Come here, play offense, we'll put you at receiver, you know this offense, you ran it.' I had a chance."

We played Houston one game in 1977 and Tony got an opportunity to play quarterback in the NFL when Terry Bradshaw and Mike Kruczek were both injured during the action. Early in the game, Tony was on defense and snared an interception. Later in the game, he was behind center and he threw an interception. Nobody else in the NFL has matched the feat yet.

COACHING POINTS

MYTHS OF FOOTBALL

▶ *Injuries Will Beat You.*

In the Super Bowl, we had injuries at running back with the Colts. Joseph Addai wasn't our top ball carrier in the Super Bowl when we beat the Bears. Dominic Rhodes got 113 yards and could've been the Super Bowl MVP. Then there was Tampa Bay vs. the Colts, the greatest comeback on *Monday Night Football*. You know who the running back was that game? Ricky Williams, a free agent from Texas Tech. We were down 35–14 with 3:42 left to go.

Tony came up to me and said, "I've seen these guys rush the passer, Tom," and I said, "We'll be okay." We scored three touchdowns and won the game 38–35. Injuries are an excuse.

He played two years at safety for us, and then we traded him to San Francisco.

Tony decided he was going to coach once his playing career was over, and he was going to the Giants. I told him to see Dan Rooney and we got that stopped.

I told Chuck the Giants were trying to hire Tony as a coach, and Chuck loved Tony because he was so smart. So he went to Dan Rooney and came back and told me to tell Tony to stop by Pittsburgh first. He never made it to New York.

Before hiring him, Chuck wanted Tony to go to the University of Minnesota and coach at the collegiate level for one year. He wanted him to get away from the Steelers and gain some experience. So he coached defensive backs for head coach Joe Salem for one year at Minnesota.

"I'd played in San Francisco for two years and I get traded again to the Giants and got cut," Dungy said. "Ray Perkins was the Giants head coach at the time, and he called me and said, 'I love the way you approach things. I think you could be a really good coach.' I talked to Tom and I said, 'I'm thinking about going with the Giants because Perkins is going to make a spot for me.' The next day, I get a call from Coach Noll. He asked, 'Are you really serious about coaching? Are you really thinking about it?' Well, yeah, I don't know what else to do. I don't think I'll get another chance to play. He said, 'Hey, you ought to come here.'

"It was really Coach Moore recruiting me again. He said, 'You'll like coaching, you'll be good at it. You'll be great, but you've got to get in the right spot. The Giants are a great organization.' Blah, blah, blah. And then the next day I got the call from Coach Noll."

A year later, I saw Tony when we hired him with the Steelers. I asked him, "What did you think of that college recruiting?" He said, "I have one good story to tell you. I'm recruiting this kid out of western Pennsylvania. I fly him in to spend the weekend, all that stuff. He flies back to Pennsylvania. I fly in and drive up one of these mountainous roads. I get to his house and he says, 'Coach, I made a decision: I'm going to Michigan.' I said, 'Okay. I understand, but I'm new—can you give me any pointers or help me by telling me, why are you going to Michigan?' He said, 'Because I like their helmets better.'"

Tony said, "And I knew college football wasn't for me."

I had known Tony since he was the eighteen-year-old recruit who was afraid to fly and had never been on an airplane and now he's on our Steelers coaching staff. That was a bigger transition for him than it was for me. He was only twenty-five and a Steelers assistant coach, the youngest in the NFL at that time.

"I'm on the staff with Tom. I'm one of the guys," Dungy said. "That was hard. It's the first time I ever called him Tom; it was always Coach Moore."

Tony eventually got used to it. All the coaches were sitting and talking about the qualifications we prized at each position one day, and we get to the safety. We're talking to Chuck, and Dungy looked up and said, "I don't know about that. I filled all those qualifications and I got traded!" And he was right.

TONY WAS AN EXCELLENT defensive backs coach. And Pittsburgh was working out for him off the field. It's where he met his beautiful wife, Lauren. She's a terrific spouse and mother. She was an elementary school teacher and today is the vice president of the Dungy Family Foundation, a best-selling author, and a motivational speaker. While things were working out for Tony in his new career, there were some people on our Steelers staff that really wanted to become head coaches and were willing to take a chance on a new league.

In 1984, the USFL was born, and Woody Widenhofer decided to take the head coaching job for the Oklahoma Outlaws. George Perles had gone to become the head coach at Michigan State two years earlier. Tony was only twenty-eight but in line to become the Steelers defensive coordinator.

The Steelers needed some youth, but probably more among the players than the coaching staff. Donnie Shell retired in 1987, and John Stallworth retired in 1987. Thankfully, it was a good draft class with players like Rod Woodson, Greg Lloyd, and Hardy Nickerson. But by 1988, after missing the playoffs for the fourth straight year, Chuck was under a lot of fire. He decided to replace Tony as defensive coordinator but keep him on the staff as the defensive backs coach. Tony decided to resign instead.

That's when Bill Parcells called me and asked if I could help him because the Giants wanted to hire Dungy. So I told Bill, yeah, I'll be happy to help because that's where I think he should go. The Giants were a great

COACHING POINTS

FIVE FOOTBALL ESSENTIALS

▶ *Postgame and End-of-Season Comments Make Me Sick.*
From the seventeenth of April until it's over, all you have to do is get better. I've heard so many fucking comments after the game. We didn't work hard enough this season. We didn't get up for this game. We didn't take this opponent seriously. I can tell you right now you've got seventeen games. Get up for them.

At the end of the season, here's what you should say: I worked as hard as I can. I prepared as hard as I can. And I played as hard as I can.

That's it. Three things. And if you can't say those things, you're stealing.

That's all you should say. None of those bullshit excuses.

organization. I told Bill, "I think you can get Tony, but you've got to recruit Lauren. I'm not sure what she thinks about living in New York." Bill Parcells thanked me.

I called Tony to tell him about Bill. I said, "You're in the media capital of the world. If you make it there—and Parcells is going to make it—you can be a head coach like that. To me, your best chance of getting exposure for what you want to do is with the Giants."

They didn't go. I don't think Lauren was very keen on beginning to raise a family in New York. I think he interviewed with the 49ers, too. I didn't think his wife would want to go there, either. Then Marty Schottenheimer hired him in Kansas City as the defensive backs coach.

I think Lauren liked Kansas City. They had a family and it made sense. Kansas City, with its middle America values, would be good for her and the kids. Marty Schottenheimer promised Tony the defensive coordinator's job if the coordinator left. That was Bill Cowher. After two seasons, Bill went to Pittsburgh as head coach, the same year that Denny Green went to Minnesota.

But Marty didn't keep his promise. He hired Dave Adolph as the defensive coordinator. That's when Tony decided to go to Minnesota as their defensive coordinator.

Denny had coached for Bill Walsh. He'd been the head coach at Northwestern. Then he went back to Bill Walsh and eventually got the Stanford job before landing with the Vikings.

Tony and I worked together the two years I was still in Minnesota with the Vikings.

Meanwhile, the Steelers defense was getting old. But mostly, I saw it as a chance to maybe become a head coach because I knew Jerry Burns would be retiring in two years. In the end, it just didn't work out.

I left in '94 to go to Detroit. I told Tony Dungy I was going to do it and that I thought he would get a head coaching job. I said, "I hope you consider me when you get a head coaching job." He said, "You know, it's probably better off if you're not here when I leave because I probably won't be allowed to take these guys."

Tony had all the credentials to lead an NFL team. I mean, in 1993, his Vikings had the No. 1 defense in the NFL. There were seven head coaching openings. But he didn't even get one damn interview.

Two years later, there were only two openings, Miami and Tampa Bay. Both teams were interested in Jimmie Johnson, the former Cowboys and University of Miami coach. The Bucs also interviewed Steve Spurrier, who decided to remain with the Florida Gators.

Meanwhile, I had gotten on with Wayne Fontes and the Lions. I was there from '94 to '96. Tony got the head coaching job in Tampa Bay and called me. Of course I would love to help him with his first NFL head coaching job. Then he called Detroit's front office to see if they would let me out of my contract. We led the league in offense. I felt they might let me go to Tampa Bay. However, Wayne Fontes wouldn't hear of it.

"I end up getting the Tampa job and I called Wayne Fontes and I said, 'Is there any way Tom Moore is available?'" Dungy said. "He said, 'I wish I could, but I can't help you on this one.'"

When Tony got the Bucs job, I couldn't have been happier. They started 1–8 in his first season but then won five of their last seven games. Warren Sapp, Derrick Brooks, and John Lynch—all eventual Hall of Famers—were coming into their own.

Even though Tony reached the playoffs four times in six years, his Bucs teams couldn't get over the hump and he was fired after the 2001 season.

By then, I had been in Indianapolis for four seasons as offensive coordinator on Jim Mora's staff. Peyton Manning was becoming a superstar. But in 2001, we were 4–4 before losing seven of our final nine games to finish 6–10. Mora was fired.

Fate would put Tony Dungy and me back together again.

The Colts hired Tony as head coach, and I couldn't have been happier for my friend.

Tony remembers the decision to maintain our offensive foundation: "Jim Irsay has already given me the job and Bill Polian comes down. We're trying to go through things, and he says, 'One thing, we don't want to dictate, but we'd really like you to keep Peyton running this offense. We'd really like you to keep Tom.' And I'm like, 'That's not a problem.' He's thinking I'm going to be all upset. This is a dream come true for me.

"When I got there, Peyton Manning is telling me, 'Pressure's what you feel when you don't know what to do,'" Dungy said. "I'm like, 'Yeah, I've heard that before.' So it's my job to get you to know what to do so you don't feel any pressure.

"It's something I learned from Chuck Noll. He told me if my guys are nervous, if they feel pressure, it's my fault because I didn't prepare them for what they had to do.

"So I'm coaching defensive backs with Coach Noll now and telling them, 'Oh, okay. So, whatever you do, guys, you can't say you're feeling under pressure!'"

Tony, Bill Polian, and Jim Irsay never really questioned any of my calls. And Tony had complete trust.

"It was so uncomfortable for me because it was total role reversal," Dungy said. "But he was the ultimate assistant coach, and that's the way he wanted it, and he was always making sure that he didn't step over my head even though I would always say, 'You know what's right.' That was hard for me because I'm thinking back to when I was eighteen years old and he'd be telling me everything and I didn't know a thing, so now I'm supposed to be in charge of making decisions? When I would have a question, I would have to go to him separately and say, 'Tom, what do you think?' And he would tell me, and of course I would go back out to the staff meeting and say, 'We're going to do this, this, and this.'

"It was just hard after all those years, but he was very professional about it and that's the way he wanted it, and both of us understood what it was like to be an assistant coach. He would humble himself much more than most people would in that situation. But those were great times. I felt so confident. I never had to worry about the offense. We're going to be fine. We're going to do the right things. We're going to be prepared. He was the perfect coach for Peyton. He would just say, 'I need to know what to do and if I know what to do, I'm going to be fine.' So Peyton had five million questions about everything that could possibly happen.

"We all knew that's not going to happen, but what if it does? Tom had all the answers for him."

It was sort of a cruel twist of fate, but the year after Tony Dungy was fired in Tampa Bay, the Bucs beat the Raiders to win Super Bowl XXXVII.

After the game, Jon Gruden was very gracious and referenced what a great job Tony had done in building that team. Their defense intercepted Raiders QB Rich Gannon five times.

The next season, Tony and our Colts returned to Tampa to play the Bucs. We were 4–0, looking to keep the streak alive. I was really fired up for that one.

The team was, too. They had so much respect for Tony, and even though he never mentioned anything about Tampa winning the Super Bowl, we all knew he had set the foundation there. He may have said, "Jon did a great job," or something like that. But there was no bitterness. No outward gripe. He never did that. He handled it like a true professional. It wasn't said out loud, but we were all thinking it: "Let's win this one, and let's win this one for Tony. Tony deserves this."

By now, Wayne Fontes was living not too far away in Tarpon Springs, and I called Wayne on the Wednesday before the game. I said, "Wayne, you coming to the game?" He said, "Yeah, I will be down there, Tom. But, Tom, I got to tell you, these guys are really good on defense." I said, "Wayne, we're going to kick their ass." He said, "But, Tom, I'm telling you, these guys are really good on defense. I'm telling you." I said, "All right, we'll see."

I walked out on the field and there was Wayne, with a big Styrofoam cup of gin and tonic or something. I said, "Wayne, how ya doing, brother? Wayne, we're about to get them." He said, "No, Tom. Unh-uh."

Not long after that, Warren Sapp ran through our pre-game warm-ups—a sign of disrespect. To this day, every time I see him I tell him, "You're lucky I didn't jack your ass up!" He just laughs.

But the game went bad. It went really bad. The Bucs were winning 35–14 with three and a half minutes to go, and that's when we started the comeback you read about it in the book's prologue.

There was a glimmer of hope, though it's always uncomfortable to pin hope on an injury. Bucs cornerback Brian Kelly got hurt. They put in Tim Wansley, who at that point was virtually a rookie.

COACHING POINTS

THINGS YOU HAVE TO GUARD AGAINST

▶ *Jealousy*

It's ruined teams. I said, "We've got Peyton Manning. We're going to throw probably about 600 passes, and he'll complete about 67 percent. So, somebody is going to catch a lot of footballs. I don't know who it's going to be. But I know it will be the guy who gets open in practice, and when he throws it to you, you've got to catch it. And if you don't get open in practice and you don't catch the sonofabitch, you're not going to see the ball in the game. It's that simple." They're all like that.

When I was in Pittsburgh, we worked as much on double coverage, because, eventually, Bradshaw was going to throw it. Tommy Prothro said, "In times of crisis, think players, not plays." If you want the ball, catch the sonofabitch but don't come to me. Catch it and you'll get all you want.

I told Marvin, "They're starting cornerback got hurt." He says, "Tom, I couldn't care less who's playing. It don't make any difference." Well, I knew that it did. And Marvin went off.

Well, at the end of the game, Marvin had 176 yards and Keyshawn had 62 yards.

This is a true story. When the score had hit 35–14, Tony said, "Tom, what do you think? I'm thinking about pulling Peyton because I've seen these guys' pass rush. They're going to tee off."

I said, "I wouldn't do it. Give us one more chance."

Tony remembers it the same way. "We're down 21 and I said, 'Tom, we've got a short week. We're going to get someone carted off if we're not careful so it might be wise to get this first group off and cut our losses.' Tom said, 'I wouldn't do that if I were you.' That's all he said, 'I wouldn't do it.'"

So, the Bucs kick off after the score and Brad Pyatt returns the ball to the Tampa Bay 17-yard line. Now it's going pretty good. We scored and Tony agrees to let me keep Peyton in. We tried an onside kick, and we recovered it. We got another possession and Marvin is wearing this rookie corner out.

What Peyton still has a hard time believing is that we had three third-down plays when we went down the field and kicked the field goal to tie it. I was concerned that the Bucs defensive coordinator, Monte Kiffin, was going to blitz. So I put both backs in the backfield in max protection. We called the same play three straight times on third down and we converted all three third downs to a different receiver and Monte never blitzed. So we went down and kicked the field goal.

It happened so fast; you didn't even realize it happened. There was 3 minutes and 42 seconds left in the game when all this started to unravel. It's still the biggest comeback in *Monday Night Football* history.

We did it against the best defense in the league.

It was Tony's birthday. His family was there.

From then on, we had confidence that we could beat anybody at any time. It was the same way I felt when I coached for Chuck Noll. The game would never be over because we had Tony.

The difference would be our coach against their coach. Oh, and we had Peyton, too.

That game was really a springboard for us.

"It told us two things," Dungy said. "That we were very good. We didn't think we were ready to compete at that level with the Super Bowl champions. And then it helped our whole team to understand, we should never doubt ourselves. Four years later, when we're in the AFC Championship Game against the Patriots and we were down 21–3 in the first half, we were like, 'We've done this in four minutes. We were going to be fine.' From that point on, it didn't matter what the score was, what the situation in the game was, we always felt like we were going to be fine.

"To me it was such a confidence boost. We did it against the best defense in football on the road when nothing was going right. But Tom had a saying that he used to tell the guys all the time before big games. It's who plays the hardest the longest, and we played just as hard as them (if not harder) the longest. They didn't play the last three and a half minutes as hard as we did, so it was vindication for that.

"Four years later when we played a great Patriots team in the AFC Championship Game and Tom says, 'It's who plays the hardest the longest,' we'd already done it."

Let's talk about that game. The Patriots had already won three Super Bowls when we hosted the AFC Championship Game at the RCA Dome on January 21, 2007. I saw Bill Belichick on the field before the game. He had said some nice things about a mutual friend in coaching who had passed away and I thanked him. Then Bill said to me, "You know, this game is the Super Bowl. We played Chicago in the regular season, and I think we really match up well against them. So this is the Super Bowl. The team that wins this game is going to win the Super Bowl."

Closer to kickoff, center Jeff Saturday gave one of the best pre-game speeches I've ever heard. He said, "We have eighteen guys with us from the 2003 AFC Championship team. Now we're getting a second chance. The other thirty-five players from that team are not with us, and they undoubtedly wish they could be here in the Conference Championship Game. This is our team and our time. I know we're going to get it done!"

Falling behind wasn't part of the plan, of course, but we knew we could come back. After Asante Samuel intercepted Manning and returned it for a touchdown, we trailed 21–3. We marched down and added a field goal, heading to the locker room trailing 21–6. It was no time for big speeches.

We stuck with the plan. Nobody panicked. We came out and scored a touchdown, driving 76 yards with Peyton Manning scoring on a quarterback sneak. We got the ball back, and when we got near the end zone, we pulled out all the stops. Peyton Manning threw a short TD pass to Dan Klecko, our defensive lineman and sometimes fullback in short yardage situations.

Our two-point conversion worked, and we tied the game 21–21.

Unfortunately, it was short-lived. Our special teams allowed the Patriots to return the kickoff 80 yards, and five plays later, Brady threw a TD pass to Jabar Gafney to lead 28–21.

After that, it was a see-saw affair. We drove back down, and Jeff Saturday pounced on a Dominic Rhodes fumble in the end zone for a touchdown.

New England kicked two field goals and we kicked one.

We were trailing 34–31 when we made our last scoring drive. It was third-and-2 on their 3-yard line, and we ran it. Jeff Saturday had the block of the century that sprung Joseph Addai for a touchdown.

But there was one minute remaining. Enough time for Tom Brady. He completed two passes and drove the Patriots across midfield to our 45-yard line. With 16 seconds to go, Marlon Jackson intercepted a pass from Brady to end the game. We were going to the Super Bowl.

I remember that when we'd left the Patriots with possession and minute to go, everybody said, "You scored too fast." I've never been a believer that you can score too fast. You score when you can score and don't worry about it.

Bill Belichick coached the Pro Bowl that year. Bill wanted to know from Peyton, "You guys were going to settle for the field goal and the tie, weren't you?"

And Peyton said, "No, we were going to whip your ass. We were going for the touchdown."

I have a picture somebody took of me sitting on the Colts bench after the game, my head in my hands. I had nothing left. I was completely spent.

The Super Bowl against the Chicago Bears was a great opportunity for Tony Dungy. He was coaching against his former Bucs assistant coach, Lovie Smith. One of them was going to be the first African American NFL head coach to win the Lombardi Trophy.

COACHING POINTS

MYTHS OF FOOTBALL

▶ *The Weather*

When I was with the Colts, we had 81 plays, 42 runs for 191 yards in the Super Bowl XLI win over Chicago, and it rained like hell the whole game. We were 25 of 38 passing for 247 yards and held the ball 38 minutes to their 22 minutes and we're playing against three of the best defensive minds in football: Lovie Smith, Ron Rivera, and Steve Wilks. The weather factor is bullshit. And we spotted them 7 points.

When Bud Grant was at Minnesota, he told them the story of when they were building the Alaska pipeline and it was cold as a sonofabitch. So, they would go out for forty-five or fifty

It rained all week, and it was a monsoon on Super Bowl Sunday at Dolphin Stadium. The Bears had a great defense and an outstanding kick returner in Devin Hester. All week long, Tony talked about not kicking the ball to Hester. Then the game started, the kick landed in the arms of Hester, and he returned the opening kickoff 92 yards for a touchdown. We're trailing 7–0 with 14:39 to go in the first quarter.

Our defense forced five turnovers that day. We took a 16–14 lead at the half and never looked back, winning 29–17. We rushed for

191 yards, with Dominic Rhodes leading the way with 113 yards and a touchdown.

"I always knew we'd have success together, but to get it validated and win it all," Dungy said, "it was great for me and not only to prove Tony Dungy can win one and Peyton Manning can win one. But also, to realize how good this guy really was and how good Tom Moore has been for all these years. To see him at the press conferences, and hear Peyton Manning talk about his offenses on a national stage, it was meaningful.

minutes and they'd come in for fifteen minutes to a half hour and then they'd go back out. One of the rigs broke down and none of those guys knew how to fix it. So, they got this Alaska Native to fix it. He came and he was out there three and a half hours. They asked, "How did you do that?" He said, "The difference between you and me is I came out here to fix the rig. You came in here to stay warm." So, when you play in inclement weather, you have to decide: Did you come to stay warm and dry, or did you come to win?

"I always think of him as kind of that old-school guy, one of six coaches on that Steelers staff. That's what I think of when I think about Tom Moore. I think of us on the staff in Pittsburgh, putting the cutups together and sitting with the video guy and taking the sixteen-millimeter film from him and cutting it and splicing it together with Scotch tape. It was whatever it takes to get the job done we're going to do and we're going to help our players be the best they can be whether it's teaching Lynn Swann and John Stallworth how to read coverages or giving Peyton Manning the confidence that we can dial up a play that we never really practiced. Tom was able to get across to that player what they needed."

When it comes to coaching, some people just have "it." Maybe I have the assistant-coach version of "it," but that's for other people to decide. My Iowa coach, Forest Evashevski, had "it." Of course Bruce Arians had "it." Chuck Noll had "it." And Tony had "it," just in a different way. It's really not for anyone to decide until after you retire.

Tony played for me. He coached with me. With the Colts, I coached for him. We won a Super Bowl together. He's one of my best friends. Believe me, I'm indebted to Tony Dungy.

8

Bruce Arians

I WAS IN BAD SHAPE after I left the Colts in 2010. Both my knees needed replacing and I was using a cane to help me get around.

But Peyton Manning's comeback from a neck injury, which forced him to miss the 2011 season, literally led to my full-time return to the NFL, as well.

It wouldn't have been possible at all, though, without Bruce Arians—one of the best coaches I've ever worked with and Peyton Manning's first quarterbacks coach on Jim Mora's Colts staff. When Manning's injury cast doubt on whether he would resume his career or retire, the Colts were ready to move on. They had gone 2–14 the year Manning was out and owned the No. 1 overall pick in the draft, which they planned to use on Stanford quarterback Andrew Luck.

Meanwhile, Mike Munchak got the head coaching job with the Tennessee Titans and wanted to hire me despite my limited mobility. I said, "Mike, I'd like to come but I have too much pride. I'm a professional. I can't give you the work you deserve. I'm just being truthful." He said, "I appreciate that."

Then Jack Del Rio called. He was the head coach in Jacksonville. I told him the same thing: "I can't do it. I'm not going to cheat you. I'm not going to steal from you. I've got too much pride. I'm a professional. I'm not a thief."

Just as Manning's comeback would start in earnest at Duke—the workout that Jeff Saturday, Dallas Clark, and Reggie Wayne also attended—little did I know that my return to the sidelines would begin there, too.

Peyton would wind up in Denver, but my future wasn't as certain.

David Cutcliffe, Duke's head coach, saw that I was hurting, so he took me in to see Duke's trainer, who said, "Let's get this thing taken care of." I said okay. He called the head guy, Duke orthopedic surgeon Dr. Michael Bolognesi. This guy is renowned for doing the best knee replacements. They x-rayed my knees and said, "Yeah, Tom, they're bad." I said, let's do it.

They did the first knee replacement in April and did the second one in August. They did so well with the first one, I was actually looking forward to getting the second surgery. That's how good they are at Duke Medical. They're phenomenal, in my opinion.

The Colts were going to play the Jaguars in Jacksonville that November, and I saw Bruce in the team hotel before the game. He asked me, "How do you feel?" I said, "I feel great. I just birdied No. 17 at TPC. I'm good to go."

"Tom comes bouncing in. I told him, 'Bro, if I ever get a head coaching job, you've got a job,'" Arians said. "I told him I might have a chance in Chicago, but if I ever get one in the NFL, you're with me. He said, 'I'm as healthy as I've ever been.'"

Bruce was on his way to winning the NFL Coach of the Year award after taking over as interim head coach for Chuck Pagano, who had to leave to battle leukemia. He should've gotten the job with the Bears, but he didn't. They hired Marc Trestman.

Then, Mike Munchak—who had fired his offensive coordinator, Chris Palmer—called me again. I went down to Nashville for the last six games, and I was like my old self. I told Bruce I knew I could do it. I said my knees were 100 percent.

And, finally, Bruce got his chance. Arizona had fired Ken Whisenhunt, and while there were several other guys Bruce had coached with in Pittsburgh on that staff, they told Bruce, "Hey, we're gone. Take the job."

Bruce Arians was already sixty when he got his shot. And he got in touch with me; he gave me the shot I needed.

Bruce remembered our meeting: "I said, 'You look great, man. You look unbelievable. . . . You're in.' I finally ended up in Arizona and we put the staff together. Tom wanted to mix veterans with youth. He wanted this young defensive line coach, Brentson Buckner. He called Todd Pratt. He said, 'Do you want to get back in?' Because he had been coaching in Japan. He's older than Tom. I brought Tom in and he's my assistant.

"First staff meeting, I said, 'These two guys forgot more football than you'll ever know. If you're smart, you'll tie yourself to the hip.' Some did, some didn't.

"When we got to Tampa Bay a few years later, and I hired Thad Lewis as our offensive assistant, I said, 'You become Tom Moore's best friend. You'll learn more football in one year than you will your whole life.'"

To me, it was a huge injustice that Bruce didn't get to be a head coach earlier. As I mentioned, he had the "it" factor. He got to the players in his own way extremely well, and he'd possessed that same damn "it" factor fifteen years earlier.

Bruce treats people well; he is fiercely loyal. That loyalty was developed early when Bruce and I became part of Jim Mora's first coaching staff in Indianapolis. In fact, he had been a tight ends coach for Mora in New Orleans in '96.

"We were at the Senior Bowl in Mobile, Alabama, when Mora was forming his staff for the Colts," Arians said. "I was with Jim Mora in New Orleans and Jim melted down. I was the tight ends coach. I was going down to the Senior Bowl. Vince Tobin with the Cardinals has a quarterbacks coaching job open, so I called Jim Mora and asked if he would recommend me.

"He said I needed to call Bill Polian, who was the general manager of the Colts at the time. I said, 'Would you recommend me to him?' He said yes. I'm driving down there to Mobile, and I get a call from Jim. 'Don't take a job,' Mora said. 'We're going to Indy. You're coaching quarterbacks.'

"Years earlier, I had gone up to the NFC scouting combine as a college coach to meet with Coach Moore and sit around and drink with the legends. I'm in awe. I had gone to Dick Hoak in Pittsburgh to get the run game. So I'm in awe of those guys just sitting around.

"Now we're back in Mobile, Alabama, and we're all sitting around talking about the Colts' staff. Bill Polian asked me, 'Who do you want?' I said, 'The best coach I've ever seen or met is Tom Moore. If you could put Tom Moore and Howard Mudd together, that would be awesome.'

"He asked me, 'Where's he at?' I said, 'He's over at the cocktail party,'" Arians said. "He said, 'Go get him.' So I found him and said, 'Coach Mora wants to meet with you.' He said, 'C'mon, let's go.'

"Jim hired him on the spot. Then we get Howard Mudd as our offensive line coach."

Writing this book solved a big mystery for me, one that lasted more than twenty-five years. I was told by Polian that Jim Mora was going to get back to me within a few days or so. I never knew why that happened *so fast,* but I'm glad it did.

BACK TO BRUCE, Peyton, and me. . . . Peyton wanted to be coached. He really took to it, and I told Bruce, "Okay, you're the quarterbacks coach and wherever Peyton is, that's where I want you. In other words, if we have backs on backers on one field and quarterbacks and wide receivers on the other field, you're wherever Peyton is. If need be, I'll go down there with the other quarterbacks, but I want that kid to have one coach."

Now, I sat in on all the quarterback meetings. I wasn't being intrusive or anything. But if something came up where you have to make a decision to do this or do that, the decision could be made by me right there. At least I knew how Peyton was being coached and what he was being told, so we were all on the same page.

When we put in the game plan, I covered the running game quickly and then the offensive line coach left. Then the rest of the game plan I put in myself, just so all these people were hearing one voice.

When we watched tape, the offensive line would do their thing. When we put in the game plan for the passing game, the receivers and quarterbacks were together because I wanted the players at each position to know what I was telling the others. You know, three people can say what means the same thing, but it doesn't come across the same way and it's confusing sometimes. If it's *one voice,* there's no doubt in my mind. Here's the deal—when things get hot, they don't fire position coaches and quality control coaches. They fire coordinators and head coaches.

Now, once we get on the field, I include anybody who sees something. I don't have all the answers on the tip of my tongue all the time. Shit, I've made mistakes and I've learned. Where you get in trouble in this business is when you stop learning, because when you do, it's over. I learn something every day.

The thing is, you've got to be willing to learn and you may learn what *not* to do, which is as important as what to do. I wanted coaches to coach. We put the game plan in together. I wanted every single coach to feel when we won, they contributed something to it. Because I've been in situations where a guy comes in and has his game plan and that's it.

"Our defense was bad," Arians said. "Bill Polian brought in Cornelius Bennett from the Bills and he's looking around the locker room saying, 'Do you guys know how good you are? You don't know how good you are?'

"He said, 'That offense is unbelievable but we're fixing the shit on this side.' And he gets no credit for it. In my opinion, Cornelius Bennett was the biggest reason we went from 3–13 to 13–3, and Peyton was growing."

A lot of people have good ideas, and you should listen to their ideas. You don't have to accept all of them.

That's where Bruce is good. When we were in Arizona, Bruce was the head coach and Harold Goodwin was the offensive coordinator and offensive line coach. Bruce put in the passing game, but he took input from the other offensive coaches.

I did the same thing with Bruce when I was in Indianapolis. Bruce had been a coordinator at Alabama. He is excellent. He knew how to handle players. He is very, very, very intelligent. People don't realize how smart Bruce is.

. . .

AFTER BRUCE GOT the Arizona job and called me, I told him I wanted it. I talked to my wife, Willie, and I said, "I don't know about you, but I'm going to Arizona."

She told me I could go if I wanted to go. She said that was fine, she totally understood. But she said she couldn't do that again. By then, she had her friends in Hilton Head. She had been there for ten years. It got to a point during my Indy years where she would come up just for the regular season. It was a good thing it was a domed stadium because she doesn't do rain games.

Right after the season, we'd go down to Hilton Head and she'd stay and any time we had four days off, I'd fly to Hilton Head. Once we left Pittsburgh, we still owned our house. A pretty nice house. We could go anywhere. My daughter got married and had a kid so I basically gave her the house in Pittsburgh, and we could come back any time we wanted.

Some time before my second-to-last season at Indy, she said, "Why don't I just come up for the games?" And I said, "Okay, why don't you just come up for the home games?" So she did.

Over the course of time, she spent more and more time in Hilton Head and that's good. She deserves it. By then, we'd been married forty-seven years.

I LEARNED A LOT from Bruce. You don't coach for Bear Bryant and not learn football. You don't play quarterback at Virginia Tech for Jimmy Sharpe and not learn football. Bruce was in it to be a football coach. He had no other agendas. Like me, he loved coaching football and was only focused on winning and making players better. Bruce was good and we worked well together.

139

I would like to think I was able to teach Bruce some things, as well.

It sounds like braggadocio, and I don't mean it to be. I don't have the ego where it's got to be all about Tom. I've always tried to boost others and will always be that way. I took Peyton to a point where he could call the whole game. That's fine. He's the show. He texted me on my eighty-fifth birthday. My text back to him was that I appreciated his greatness and his friendship.

Like I said, we helped each other. Bruce and I helped each other, too.

"To coach with Tom, it was complex but the simplest offense ever," Arians said. "Receivers don't switch sides and you get on the edge of those numbers. Peyton can see those numbers. If the DBs are outside, we'll throw it inside. If they're inside, we'll throw it outside. If they got eight in the box, we're throwing it over them, and if it's Cover 2, we're running it. It's always three plays: two runs and a pass.

"I'm like, 'This is amazing.' Now I know why Barry Sanders, Cris Carter, all those guys had great years. This is unbelievable. For me, I thought I was a pretty good coach and then Tom trusted me to put in some stuff. He said, 'Give me your best eight pass plays.' I drew them all up and showed him how we read them. They're in. You teach Peyton. Each week, we'd come up with three or four things on third down. He'd ask, 'What do

COACHING POINTS

THINGS YOU HAVE TO GUARD AGAINST

▶ *Agendas*

People have their own agendas. Players that are just out for themselves or looking out for their own contract. Assistant coaches who have their own agendas to become a head coach. When those things permeate a coaching staff and a team, you're in trouble.

you got?' Now I'm into it and growing as a coach. I'm saying, 'Coach, I think we can get this corner on this and the play-action stuff. Then there's these naked bootlegs. Then we've got to throw it in the flat—what if we block this guy?' Then Howard Mudd would say, 'Yeah, but we've got to turn one of the guys loose.' Then we can throw it down the field.

"We started going with this hard play-action and we taught Peyton to set the hook with the ball fake. Got that from Steve DeBerg. I took all of Steve's film from Kansas City and showed Peyton and told him, 'You've got to put the football in your left hand and show them the ball.' It's called setting the hook. Later, we put a video together to show young quarterbacks how to play. They used it on the *ManningCast* the other night.

"I grew so much as a coach and being with Howard Mudd, who simplified the running game so much. You got a tight end that can block, you can run the football. I didn't know anything about counts. I was a power guy, trap option and a wishbone quarterback. But the best passes I ever had as a wishbone quarterback were full flow throwbacks. That's where let's bootleg this way and throw it back the other way comes from. We started lighting everybody up."

After a couple years, Peyton knew what I was going to call before I called it. I gave him more control of the offense. If I hadn't, it would've been an injustice. He could handle it and he deserved that kind of autonomy and recognition. In other words, when people think of the Indianapolis Colts, they think of Peyton Manning. They don't say Tom Moore. And that's okay. I don't really give a shit. Because Peyton's the young gun who deserves it. I tell people about this or that, they say, "Yeah, but you had Peyton." Oh no, no, no, no. I had Bubby Brister and Mark Malone . . . I had a bunch of them. I learned how to win with quarterbacks who were not headed to the Hall of Fame back in Pittsburgh.

Lynn Swann told Chuck one time, "Thanks be to God for Tom Moore." And that quotation ran in some newspapers. Well, look at the passing stats before I got there and then after. We definitely got better. But if he did say that, he ought to know that I said thanks be to God for Swann, Stallworth, and Bradshaw.

To quote Chuck, that's what I was supposed to do. You're supposed to make them great. That's your job. And there were a lot of people involved. It wasn't just me. To be great, you've got to want to be great. It's got to be burning within you. For all the great ones, it's a burning sensation inside of you.

Like Bradshaw. He called all his own plays at Pittsburgh, and he won four Super Bowls. That was Chuck's philosophy. You're the coach, yes, but this game is for the players. Make the players great. That's why Chuck, God rest his soul, never took one single dime of the players' money for endorsement deals or anything like that. He would say, "Don't take the players' money. Let them have it."

You're not in it for the money. You're in it to make those guys be successful. That's my greatest thrill in football, watching those guys succeed during and after.

It took Chuck Pagano getting sick, unfortunately, for Bruce Arians to have an eleven-week audition as head coach in Indianapolis to prove he could do it. The thing I always tried to guard against is thinking you're not a success if you never get to be head coach.

Bruce did a heck of a job in Arizona. We had some good players there, like Larry Fitzgerald, and added to them. The big move was the trade with the Raiders for quarterback Carson Palmer. He passed for a career-high 4,274 yards in 2013. He was an excellent quarterback. Big arm. Very tough.

We finished with a 10–6 record, doubling the win total from 2012. It was only the second time in thirty-seven years that the Cardinals had at least 10 wins. We were in playoff contention until the final week of the season.

"I'm loyal to probably a problem, but Tom Moore raised me in this business," Arians said. "I thought I was a pretty good coach, but I became a coach watching him. And for advice, I lean on him so much. In Arizona, I had this suite with this bar. I would say to Tom Moore and Tom Pratt, 'When this meeting is over, come to my apartment.' They're drinking their Chardonnay, and I would ask, 'What do you think?' They might say, 'We're being too easy on them.' I would say, 'All right, we'll kick their ass tomorrow.' Next day, I would ask, 'What do you think?' They would say, 'Great practice. I think I would ease off just a little bit tomorrow.'

"I just depended on them so much because they'd seen it all. I'd say, 'Tom, what do you think of this guy?' He would say, 'Carson can do this, but you've got to watch that.'"

The second year, Carson tore his ACL. We turned to Drew Stanton, who played well but also became injured. Ryan Lindley finished it up. We lost to Carolina in the wildcard game.

Palmer's third year in Arizona was his best, passing for 4,671 yards and 35 touchdowns. But we lost in the NFC Championship Game to Carolina. Palmer threw 4 interceptions. He also lost 2 fumbles.

* * *

IT WAS NICE OUT THERE in Phoenix. It was a good place, but it's like a lot of the southern cities. You play Green Bay and you've got to use the silent count on offense because you've got a lot of screaming Green Bay people there at the game in Arizona. In Arizona, basically, everybody's from somewhere else. But that's okay. It was good and the support staff was good.

Then, Bruce developed some health issues and decided to retire after going 8–8 in 2017.

He wasn't out of football for long. He spent the 2018 season calling NFL games for CBS as a color analyst. It was a lot of travel and he discovered he was having to work nearly as hard as he did as a coach preparing for games and traveling each week.

But that the gig didn't scratch his itch.

2018 was the longest year of my life. The Cardinals hired Steve Wilks as head coach, and he brought in his own coaching staff. I was back in Hilton Head. I got tired of watching the NFL RedZone. All you can do is be envious of everybody else who is working. I never gave up hope. I'm indebted to Bruce because that's what my life is—coaching and competing. I love to compete.

A couple things fell into place. The Bucs were making a change at head coach. Bruce had worked several years in Arizona with Jason Licht, now the Bucs general manager.

Bruce has always said he wouldn't have come back to coaching unless he could get his guys back. It just so happened that we were all available: Todd Bowles, Byron Leftwich, Harold Goodwin, Nick Rapone, Clyde Christensen, Kevin Ross. He was able to put the band back together.

I'm very appreciative of the people in the Bucs organization, very thankful to the Glazer family ownership. How many people are going to keep a guy who is over eighty years old around? I mean, really? There's got to be some guardian angels watching over me. People don't understand what it's like when you're eighty-five, to have a job and to go to work every day. They don't understand how great that feeling is.

Bruce Arians, in my book, is one of the greatest people in the world because he gave this Tom Moore character in his seventies an opportunity to coach another ten years. That's what friends are about. When you pick friends, you pick people. I have two criteria. Who would you want to raise your kids and who would you like to be on the *Titanic* with? I'd let Bruce Arians raise my kids and I'd go on the *Titanic* with him any time he wants to go on a cruise. But one thing in coaching: Don't ever take advantage of your friendship. When you come into the building, he's the head coach and you're the assistant.

WE HAD OUR WORK cut out for us when Bruce and company took over the Bucs in 2019. Jameis Winston was in his fifth and final season, and if anybody could salvage the Bucs' former No. 1 overall pick, it would be Bruce. A lot of us wish we could've had another year with Jameis, who worked really hard at it. But after throwing 30 interceptions, breaking Peyton Manning's record as a rookie, Bruce and Jason Licht felt they owed it to the Glazer family to see "what was behind Door No. 2," as they said.

Nobody knew that player would be Tom Brady.

After Tom joined us, COVID hit and that disrupted everything. As I mentioned earlier, Tom Brady couldn't work out with his new teammates at the facility.

I don't think Bruce can get enough credit for the job he did in 2020 when we won the Super Bowl. But as I told him, the team that beats the virus is going to win it all.

The Glazers did every single thing to help us. We had a testing lab in our parking lot. And we had advantages other teams didn't have.

"We sign Tom Brady, and we can't meet. Blaine Gabbert and those guys are going over to Berkeley Prep and putting the offense in. 'Hey, I like this, I like that,' Blaine is telling me. 'He likes this or that and I'm learning, too.'"

Bruce turned out to be the biggest enforcer when it came to all the COVID-19 protocols.

"A big part of our success also belonged to our owners," Arians said. "We built those outdoor meeting rooms. Thank God we could roll the doors up because the field house was considered outdoors. I could do all my meetings. I think we had a big advantage. I did one Zoom call all year."

There's also a funny story about how Bruce made everyone know he was serious, and it happened as soon as we began preparing for the season.

"Here's how the whole thing started, and word got around fast," Arians said. "The elevator comes up in the facility. They just put the sign up, 'One person at a time.' One of the PR directors, Mike Pehanich, and Rob Gronkowski get off the elevator together. I blew a gasket. You motherfuckers can't read? That sign says one person! There's the fucking stairs right there! We don't beat this fucking disease, we ain't beating nobody!

"Then, I calmly said, 'Glad to have you, Gronk,' as I got on the elevator. He said, 'Nice to meet you, Coach,' as he passed me getting out of it. He went down to the locker room and let everybody know I just ripped his ass. But the guys bought in. They were so good. And then the owners just kept building stuff. We got Brady. Keep building. Whatever it takes. Our weather permitted us to do things outside. Other teams around the league, in Green Bay and Minnesota, were meeting on Zoom all year."

Tom Brady raised everybody's game. But after a good start, we were 8–5 and trailed the Atlanta Falcons 17–0, fighting for our playoff lives.

Brady led us to scores on every possession in the second half until a punt with less than 3 minutes remaining. He passed for a season-high 390 yards and 2 touchdowns.

We changed some things in our protection and got on a run but had to go on the road in the playoffs. We won in Washington and New Orleans.

"Then we've got to go play at Green Bay and they're hanging the Super Bowl banners over at Raymond James Stadium," Arians said. "I was like, 'Hey, boys. I know everybody drives that way. If you're looking at those fucking banners, we're going to get our ass kicked this week. We ain't in that game. We've got Green Bay. Get your ass ready.' That scared the crap out of me. They bought in."

It all came down to a couple of plays before halftime and the end of the game. With no time-outs and eight seconds remaining in the first half, we had the ball at the Green Bay 39-yard line.

COACHING POINTS

MYTHS OF FOOTBALL

▶ *Number of Plays*

You're going to have 8 possessions and a chance to score 56 points. Maybe you only had 35 plays, but you got 8 possessions. Maybe as few as 6.

So, you can score 42 points. You'll win most games. So shut up.

One year, we played the Dolphins in Miami on Monday Night Football and had 38 plays and beat them 27–23. Now, it helped that we threw a touchdown pass on the first play of the game.

"We could've kicked that field goal. I said, 'Fuck it, let's go for it!'" Arians said. "They thought we were going to throw a quick out or something."

Instead, Brady threw deep to Scotty Miller for a 39-yard touchdown to give us a 21–10 lead at halftime and all the momentum. "Eight go," Arians said of the play. "Tom put it right on the money. Game over."

Well, almost. We didn't play well offensively in the second half. Tom Brady threw 3 interceptions. The Packers had first-and-goal at our 8-yard line. Three incompletions later, Matt LeFleur decided to kick the field goal. They never got the ball back.

COACHING POINTS

MYTHS OF FOOTBALL

▶ *Bad Referees Will Get You Beat.* Win in spite of them. Don't be intimidated. You can overcome bad calls.

We picked up three first downs, helped by a pass interference penalty against Kevin King on Tyler Johnson. That let us run out the clock.

"I think Matt LeFleur did the right thing in the fourth quarter kicking the field goal," Arians said. "They had four time-outs when you think about it. They had three and the two-minute warning."

On third and 5, Byron Leftwich called for Chris Godwin to run a sweep around right end. He picked up 6 yards and slid down in bounds. We were headed home to play in Super Bowl LV.

"We had that five wideout package with that crack sweep to Chris," Arians said. "He hadn't run it all year. I said, 'Byron, it's time for the crack sweep.' He said, 'Coach, I love it.' That's one of the few times I ever called a play in Tampa. Chris Godwin runs the crack sweep and game over."

. . .

THE KANSAS CITY CHIEFS were defending Super Bowl champs. We had played Kansas City earlier in the year and Tyreek Hill had touchdowns of 75, 44, and 20 yards that day. He finished with 13 catches for 269 yards, but we made it close, losing 27–24.

The Super Bowl was a different story. Todd Bowles had a brilliant game plan, rushing four and playing coverage to keep everything in front of us. We sacked Patrick Mahomes three times and intercepted him twice.

"We had played Kansas City earlier in the year and Tyreek got behind us," Arians said. "That wasn't happening again. Our pass rushers chased Mahomes all over the field. Everyone said we blitzed him. No, we didn't blitz him. We came after him with our front four. We put Vita Vea and Ndamukong Suh on the outside and Jason Pierre-Paul and Shaquil Barrett on the inside and they crushed their tackles. They didn't score a touchdown."

This shows how Bruce held everyone accountable. Ronald Jones was our starting tailback and nearly rushed for 1,000 yards but missed the last two games of the regular season with COVID-19. Then he pulled a quad muscle before the playoff game at Washington and couldn't go. We turned to Leonard Fournette, who had just an amazing postseason, earning the nickname Playoff Lenny.

But there had been a point during the season when Leonard didn't accept his backup role and was sulking. Bruce took care of it.

"That was a come to Jesus meeting," Arians said. "He's sitting on the cooler back there at practice. I rode back there on my cart and said, 'What's the problem? I love you. But you've got thirty minutes. Go call whoever you've got to call. You come back here and tell me to cut you or you're all in. I'll cut you right now. No problem.'

"He came back and said, 'I'm in.' I said, 'Good, get your ass in there.' And he engaged. He became Playoff Lenny."

Fournette's 27-yard touchdown run in the third quarter of the Super Bowl put the game away. "He got that carry on a play that was actually RoJo's play," Arians said. "It was a speed play. Lenny wasn't getting caught. As soon as Ali Marpet pulled, Lenny wasn't getting caught. I didn't know it was over. I didn't breathe until Devin White got that interception to end the game. I knew Mahomes could score so fast, and he was throwing shit upside down and hitting people in the face mask."

I had won my fourth Super Bowl ring and I owe it to Bruce and the Glazers for allowing me to coach in Tampa Bay. A lot of good players were here and had not been to a playoff game. Now, they had won four postseason matchups and were Super Bowl champs.

"To see Mike Evans's face. Lavonte David's face. It was unbelievable," Arians said. "It was the greatest feeling a coach could have. Lavonte hit me so hard, I thought he tore my rotator cuff. Suh. JPP [Jason Pierre-Paul]. I mean, I love JPP. He said, 'We did it!' Toughest guy I ever coached. That's my guy. I loved that guy. To play with the MCL and the shoulder. He couldn't lift his arm. And he'd practice once a week. I said, 'You don't have to practice, bro.' He said, 'I have to. I have to learn my shit. His heart bled through that team and Suh has a big one, too. He led a totally different way. He managed Vita Vea. He kept his weight down. Suh was on his ass."

There's nothing like winning a Super Bowl. What made this one different, more incredible, was to do it during a pandemic, when our families couldn't really have any interaction with each other.

"You know, as a coach, I think as a kid, you dream about that fucking Gatorade bath," Arians said. "It still shocked me, but it was the greatest feeling of my career. And no one would give me a towel. I'm on the podium and I'm soaking wet. My wife, Chris, is asking, 'Why are you so wet?' We had a family hug. That's the best hug ever."

After the ceremony, most of our locker room had cleared out. Because of COVID-19, the league didn't really want us to have a Super Bowl party. Thank God for Darcie Glazer Kassewitz, who had one for us anyway at the Florida Aquarium in Tampa.

"You don't even get to have a team meeting after the game," Arians said. "I go into the locker room and nobody is there. There's just smoke. Cigars everywhere. I'm like, 'What the hell?' The buses were leaving."

Bruce said he had a box of Arturo Fuente cigars sent to him. "I thought they jinxed me because it said 'Super Bowl winners' on the box. "Black onyx. Beautiful box," Arians said. "I get on the bus; I'm throwing around cigars. We get to the Aquarium, my little brother says, 'Quit throwing out those cigars. They're like $150 apiece. You can't buy these.'"

I owe a lot to Bruce Arians for allowing me to continue to live my dream. In his own way, I told Bruce he reminded me of Chuck Noll.

"It's the greatest compliment I've ever received," Arians said. "And I cried. It meant so much to me.

"I mean, to put my name next to Chuck Noll, who I still think is the greatest coach ever? What he did with the Steelers, taking them from nothing to winning four Super Bowls? Tom said, 'You're a great coach. You're right there with Chuck Noll.' I mean, I literally cried."

9

Barry Sanders, the Lion King

BARRY SANDERS, the Lion King, used to fall asleep in the film room. When we turned out the lights and rolled tape, the Lion slept. This happened so often that I finally said, "Damn it, Barry, you've got to stay awake."

Barry replied, "I know, Tom. But what I see on that screen is not what I see on that field."

"Well, that's interesting," I said. "Explain that to me."

He said, "Every game starts fast, but the more I carry the ball, the slower the game gets."

His production proved that. Most games, he'd carry the ball the first 15 times for about 35 yards. But he'd finish the game with 28 carries for 175 yards. It's interesting. One year I think he had six runs of more than 65 yards and didn't score.

"That was the key. He made more short-yard runs than anybody, but he made more long runs than anybody in the league," said Wayne Fontes, who was the Lions head coach from '88 through '96, including my years there. "And he made the short runs exciting."

I worked with Wayne Fontes at Dayton when he coached the defense with George Perles, and we had some great intra-squad battles. He left to become an assistant coach at Iowa and somehow got hooked up with Southern Cal coach John McKay. When McKay became the head coach of the expansion Tampa Bay Buccaneers, Fontes worked as an assistant with Abe Gibron on defense before eventually taking his job as defensive coordinator.

When McKay retired from the Buccaneers at the end of the '84 season, Fontes went to Detroit as the defensive coordinator under head coach Monte Clark. When they fired Monte, it was all kind of set up for Wayne to take over the Lions because he was in good with their owner, Mr. William Clay Ford Sr. But Mr. Ford went out and hired Darryl Rogers. After a couple of losing seasons, the Lions started 2–9 in 1988, and Rogers wondered aloud, "What does a coach have to do around here to get fired?"

He had done enough, and Mr. Ford turned to Wayne Fontes to take over as head coach.

I was in Pittsburgh at the time and Wayne talked to me, but he couldn't hire me because the Lions were enamored with the run-and-shoot offense, something I wasn't known for. He was stuck. He had to keep that.

So I went to Minnesota and was there two years hoping I would get the Vikings head coaching job when Jerry Burns retired. It didn't happen. Denny Green came in as head coach and kept me as the Vikings receivers coach. He was good to me. Eventually, Brian Billick became the offensive coordinator, and it was obvious to me he wanted to select his own receivers coach, and that was fine.

If you're not wanted, you find another job, and I did. I joined Wayne Fontes in Detroit.

There's never been a more exciting running back I've coached than Barry Sanders. Franco Harris and Edgerrin James were great. They're also in the Pro Football Hall of Fame. But Barry Sanders was spectacular.

His ability to make people miss tackles was probably second to none.

When I was with the Vikings, we had a safety named Joey Browner. Joey said when he played Barry, he never tried to square him up for a tackle. He waited until Barry got by him and tried to tackle him from behind because Barry couldn't see him to make him miss.

I will never forget one game we were playing Pittsburgh in 1995, and the Steelers were leading 3–0. It was third down and Barry took a swing pass to the left. I can see it in my mind as I write about it. Rod Woodson came up to make a tackle and never touched him. What's worse, the move Barry put on him to make him miss tore up Rod's knees. That was the end of Woodson's cornerback days. He had to move to safety after that game.

Whatever the situation, you could put the football in Barry Sanders's hands and know he was going to find a way to make a play.

"We're playing Minnesota and it's fourth-and-1 and we're at our own 35-yard line with maybe one minute to go in the game," Fontes said. "I think we're up by two. The punt team came running onto the field. Everybody would've punted it. Tom walks up to me and the offensive linemen are coming off the field and they said, 'Coach, we can make this.'

"So I call time-out. I said, 'You know what? If we go for it and make a first down, they've got no chance. The game is over.

If we go for it on fourth down and don't get it, they're going to get good field position and we're going to lose the game.' I kept going back and forth. Tom said, 'We're going to make it.' I remember our safety, Bennie Blades, came up to me and said, 'If we don't make it, we'll stop them!'

"I said, 'Let's go for it!'

"Now my defensive coaches are going crazy. We get the snap and I looked at the formation and they had eleven guys on the line of scrimmage. Nobody is covering the wideout. I mean, he was so wide open, but they knew Barry was going to get the ball. They've got nine on the line and two guys sort of shading over to the wide receivers. Barry takes one step, three yards deep, and gets hit. He goes flying backward. I said, 'Oh Jesus, we're going to lose this game.'

"He does a spin, lands back on his feet, turns around, and starts running to his left. Now, when he runs to his left, it seems like they've got nineteen guys over on that side of the field. So he stops, cuts back the other way, and it's like there's another nineteen guys waiting for him. He stops, plants, leaps over the middle, and he gets hit. Remember those little propeller hats? He spun around like one of those propellers and I thought, 'Oh, Jesus. It's going to be so close.' The referees called time-out for a measurement. They came out to get a good look at the spot and they had to get a card and push it down to see if they could get any space between the football and the yard marker. Then they yelled, 'First down!'

"I said, 'Let's take a knee and end the damn game.' When we're going to the locker room after the game, I can barely breathe. I thought I was going to get fired on this call. When we made it, the team had come up to me and gave me one of those Gatorade baths.

"We're going in and Tom came up to me and said, 'I told you we were going to make it.'"

That's the kind of trust we had in Barry and the trust Wayne Fontes had in me.

AT THE END OF BARRY'S ROOKIE YEAR, he was about five yards short of the rookie rushing record. The Lions are beating the other team, so Wayne pulls him. When he pulled him, somebody sent a note down to Wayne from the press box: "Hey, he needs something like five yards to break the rookie rushing record." So Wayne went over and asked, "Barry, you need five yards to get the rookie rushing record. Do you want to go back in?" And Barry shook his head and said, "Let the other guy have it."

In '94, the Lions had their running back, for sure, but we needed a quarterback and went into the free agent market. The big question if you needed a quarterback that year was, do you sign Scott Mitchell or do you sign Warren Moon? Well, Mitchell was twenty-six and Moon was already thirty-eight.

Mitchell was young and coming off a good year with the Dolphins. Warren Moon was good. He'd been there. But we opted to sign Scott Mitchell, and the Vikings took Warren Moon. We also signed quarterback Dave Krieg, who was thirty-six but could light you up if he got hot.

"Tom will tell you straight up, you have to have players to win," Fontes said. "When he went to Pittsburgh, they had a great team. Later, after he left us and went to Indianapolis, he had Peyton Manning. He said, 'You need players to win.'

"Tom Moore outcoached everybody. He never had all the talent everybody else had in Detroit. You can look at all the great coaches. When they lose the guy under center, they can't win a game. Now you come out and say, 'You can't win without players.' But when a coach gets fired from Dallas, Detroit, or wherever it is, it's always the coach's fault.

"Bill Belichick, Don Shula, and Jimmy Johnson—there were none better. But when they lost a key player, they were just like everybody else. That's Tom's deal. Coaches coach great players.

"The thing about Tom, he took players that maybe the other coaches couldn't have and made winners out of them. That's the best thing I can say about him."

I was very, very involved with Scott Mitchell and trying to sign him. I liked everything I saw on the tape with the limited time he played with the Dolphins. I pushed for him. Wayne and Dave Levy and I went down to Ft. Lauderdale and spent a day with him and recruited him hard. I think he's gotten a bad rap to this day, to tell you the truth.

The game management, the audibles and stuff like that, he handled extremely well.

That first year, Dave Levy called the runs, and I called the passes on offense while coaching quarterbacks. We started 2–1. The highlight was a showdown between Barry Sanders and Dallas running back Emmitt Smith in Dallas on *Monday Night Football*. We won the game, 20–17 in overtime. It was a big deal to our offensive linemen that Sanders outplayed Emmitt. Barry may have won the day, rushing 40 times for 194 yards. Smith went for 143 yards and a touchdown on 29 carries.

"We had a fundamentally sound blocking scheme in the run game," tackle Lomas Brown said. "We would trip out. There's five of us and they would bring up a sixth guy and we wouldn't change out the play. Tom would tell you, 'Leave the play on.' He would tell Barry in the meetings, 'Barry, this free guy? That's your guy.' Nine out of ten times, he'd get the ball and he'd be able to shake him. Was that normal? No, it wasn't. But again, we had the greatest running back in the game, and why not utilize his skills?

"For us, it was imperative we came out on top. If you remember, it was Dallas and Detroit, two young teams that were going to be the up-and-coming teams, especially after the '91 season. We beat them to go to the NFC Championship Game. . . . Anytime we played those guys, we always wanted to make sure Barry was the guy who came out on top because we knew Barry was a better pure running back. Emmitt was a guy who had more help, but we always felt Barry was the best running back and we always wanted to make sure that was displayed each and every time we played those guys.

"That was big for us, and it was a *Monday Night Football* game. We wanted the fans to know what type of team we had. The only way to do that was to play against the best and beat the best."

We lost our next three games but finished strong, going 9–7 and earning a wildcard playoff spot. Mitchell got hurt and we had to turn to Dave Krieg in the playoffs, losing to the Packers 16–12. Sanders was held to minus-1 yard rushing in the game because the Packers dared us to throw the football and we weren't good enough that day.

I took over all the play-calling duties the next year, but we started 0–3. The natives were getting restless. On offense, we were trying to do some things with motion to create mismatches in the secondary. The players had a players-only meeting. Some of the offensive linemen were complaining about some of the zone blocking schemes. I think a receiver or two spoke up. I asked Barry what he thought of the meeting, and he said, "That was the biggest waste of time. Let's just do what the coaches say."

"Tom was always a calming influence," Brown said. "The reason I say that is his voice was always the same. You'd never see him get excited. You probably could never tell whether we were up or down in a game based on his expressions. He was always just one way. I always thought, as a player, when you don't see your coach going up and down, I think that helps you not to panic and not to overreact to things. It was almost like a grandfather figure for us as a team along with being an excellent, excellent offensive coordinator and an innovative guy. He was once one of the most innovative guys in the league. All these new coaches came in with things that Tom did."

I knew we had to run plays based on the skills of our players. I remember saying, "Here's what we're going to do. Who's our best people?" We had Herman Moore, Brett Perriman, and Johnnie Morton at receiver. So we went three wideouts and that was it. It was 2 x 2, with two receivers on either end of the line of scrimmage; or 3 x 1, with three receivers on one side and one on the other end of the line of scrimmage. That was it. No motion. We ran where they ain't. If the defense was loaded left, we ran right. If they were lined up more to the right, we ran left. Simple.

If they were doubling two guys, that means there's a one-on-one somewhere. Now, that's an oversimplification but that's essentially what we did, and we ran off 10 wins and had the best offense in the NFL.

"All the quarterbacks we had in that system, I will say the one thing Tom did was give them freedom to come up and change the play," Brown said. "That was huge for a quarterback to be able to come up there and be able to change plays like that and Tom giving them the confidence and also giving them what they needed to be able to change plays by having other plays you could go to. To me, he was just great and ahead of his time."

As for Barry? He was going to go wherever he wanted to. He'd tell the offensive linemen, "If you can't block them, get out of the way and I'll make them miss."

With Barry, we used all zone blocking and draw blocking. We had a couple different types of draws—a sprint draw and a regular drop-back draw. But it was all zone and draw blocking. You wanted to hand Barry the football and let him decide where he wanted to run.

We had San Francisco on *Monday Night Football* in 1995. They were defending Super Bowl champions. We had started 0–3 and the pressure was building. I remember Hank Stram, who was calling the game, came up to me and asked, "What are you going to do, Tom?" I told him, "Get ready because we're going to throw a lot of bombs." And we beat them 27–24. That game was prefaced by that players-only meeting. That's really when we decided to go with three receivers. Nobody moves. Nobody gets hurt. Read the defense and take what they give you.

Our Lions offense produced the first-ever tandem of 100-catch receivers in '95—Moore and Perriman. Only two teams have ever had a 4,000-yard passer, a 1,500-yard rusher, two 1,000-yard receivers . . . and Perriman was just 12 yards shy of racking up 1,500 for the season. (Our 1999 Colts team would be the second team to do it, four years later.)

We played a Saturday game and had to beat the Bucs to get into the 1995 playoffs. We had the game locked up. I always ask the players, "What do you need for incentives and stuff?" I'm talking about benchmarks in their contracts that earn them salary bonuses. That kind of thing. We get to the last drive and all we have to do is get a first down and flop on it and the game is over. But stupid me, Herman needed four receptions to break the single season record. I told Scott Mitchell, "We're going to throw four passes and I want them all to go to Herman." So we called four passes and got four completions to Herman. That gave him 122 receptions. He got the record.

So now we're down to the 8-yard line. It's the two-minute warning and Tampa Bay is out of time-outs. We could take a knee and the game is over. Brett Perriman comes over to me and says, "Tom, I only need 25 yards to get my bonus." I said, "Brett, we're on the 8-yard line!" He said, "Well, call a pass and tell Scott to take a sack." I said, "No, Brett, we're not doing that one, I'm sorry."

There's only so much you can reasonably do.

HERMAN MOORE set the NFL single-season receptions record. Cris Carter played the next day, on Sunday, and wound up with 123 catches, one shy of Herman, and he was hot! You can't believe how hot they both were.

Record set, one bonus missed, and we made our way to the playoffs. We played the Eagles in the NFC wildcard and were one and done again, allowing the Eagles to score 31 points in the second quarter, and 58 overall. Scott Mitchell had a tough day, throwing 4 INTs and we lost a fumble.

Scott was a smart quarterback who understood the game. He handled the huddle and pre-snap adjustments extremely well. But here's the deal. I was the offensive coordinator, and I'd been an officer in the US Army. In the military, you learn very, very quickly that you can delegate authority but not responsibility. I was responsible for the results on offense. Don't blame him, blame me. Because, obviously, I did a horseshit job of preparing him or whatever went wrong that caused the interceptions would not have happened. That's what I believe and that's how I feel.

It's my responsibility. You have a responsibility and you've got to own up to it. A lot of people want authority, but then when it comes to the responsibility, they start looking for corners to hide in. I'm not that way.

Don't blame Scott Mitchell for the interceptions, blame me.

"It's very, very difficult—very—in the National Football League to win without a top quarterback," Fontes said. "You can lose with a top quarterback, but it's very difficult to win without one.

"When we were at Detroit, I guess the people in the press didn't really believe that. We never had a top-flight quarterback there. They were good. Yet, they weren't at the level that Tom Moore had when he was at the Pittsburgh Steelers. But the thing I want to say to that is he took our offense—and we had a good team, we had Barry Sanders—but we needed a guy under the gun. We didn't really have that guy. But if you go back and see what Tom Moore did with that offense.

"The year he really shined was when the Detroit Lions offense led all passing categories. Tom had a great mind. The quarterback knew where to go with the football. The receivers knew what to do when the ball got there. He had so much detail."

After the playoff loss to the Eagles, we came back the next year and we were feeling better about ourselves. But in that first week of training camp, Scott was served divorce papers. It affected him. Then we had some injuries. As a starter, Mitchell went 4–10 with 17 touchdown passes and 17 interceptions.

Barry was always very, very protective of Wayne, and he used to tell the reporters and columnists to get off Wayne's back. In return, Wayne Fontes covered for Barry during minicamps. They had an arrangement where Barry would come the first day and then Wayne would excuse him and tell the media he had to leave for some personal reason.

Barry was like Edgerrin. "You know these voluntary workouts?" Edgerrin would say. "I know I went to the U, and I've got gold teeth, but I know the difference between voluntary and mandatory." Well, so did Barry. But don't worry about Barry's conditioning. I had seen Barry after practice on Wednesday and Thursday running gassers by himself just to get into shape.

WHEN I LEFT MINNESOTA for Detroit, I figured Tony Dungy would get a head coaching job soon. It finally happened in 1995 and he called the Lions and Wayne Fontes to see if they would let me go to Tampa Bay to be his offensive coordinator.

"Of course I wanted Tom to be my offensive coordinator in Tampa, but Wayne wouldn't entertain it and I understood why. He made everybody the best they could be. Whatever you had, he was going to get it out of you. And it was so fundamentally sound. There were no frills. No bells and whistles. People would tell you this isn't the Scott Mitchell they've ever seen before. It was just Scott Mitchell putting up yards.

"That was Tom's brilliance. Everybody thinks you have to do this, this, and this. But no, his guys don't need to do all that. He says, 'This can be effective for us and we're doing it.' You can't necessarily explain it to anybody else. It doesn't make sense."

Just as perplexing was Barry Sanders calling it quits when he did.

Barry was a very proud person. He worked very hard. But he was so loyal to coaches. There's a lot of speculation, but all of a sudden he said, "That's it." I've heard him say he didn't regret it.

He wasn't a lifer like me. That's okay.

It's like his first year when he needed only a few yards to win the rookie rushing title. It would have meant a lot to the Lions, even more to his offensive linemen.

"Man, we begged Barry," tackle Lomas Brown said. "You want to go back in?"

He just said it wasn't important to him.

Barry Sanders played ten seasons. His dad was a passionate fan who believed Jim Brown was the best running back who ever lived. Barry did everything in his power to be the best, even in his dad's eyes. He certainly made the Lions relevant again and helped restore the roar.

His retirement was understated. He faxed a letter to the Lions and boarded a plane to London. He had passed Jim Brown in career rushing yards but retired only 1,457 yards shy of Walter Payton's NFL record at the time, since eclipsed by Emmitt Smith and Frank Gore. Maybe running down his dad's idol was enough.

"You kind of knew," Lomas Brown said. "And the thing I knew is that, once he retired, he wasn't coming back. You heard all those rumors. Maybe he'll come back. Maybe he'll go to another team. That's how Barry was. He would always stick to his convictions, whatever they were. It didn't shock us. In '95, they let me and Chris Spielman leave. Then two years later, they let Kevin Glover and Bennie Blades leave. I think that's when Barry knew. It was never the same team anymore."

Wayne Fontes was fired after the 1996 season and Bobby Ross took over. The Lions made the playoffs again, but they lost to the Bucs in Tampa in the NFC wildcard game. My good friend Tony Dungy had won his first postseason game.

I think had they given us more time, Scott would've come around and done a great job. I'm still in Scott Mitchell's corner.

I think he did a lot of good things. I think he had a promising future. But then they let Wayne go. They let all of us go and whatever happened, happened.

I NEEDED ANOTHER JOB, and I was on my way to New Orleans. I agreed with Mike Ditka to become the Saints running backs coach.

Shortly after accepting the job, I was in New Orleans with the Saints' new coaching staff. The city was hosting the Super Bowl, and we were staying at the Hilton near the airport. I got a call from Raiders head coach Joe Bugel, who wanted to hire me as the Raiders offensive coordinator.

It was a great opportunity, but like I told Bugel, I had already given my word to Ditka and I wasn't going back on my word. Bugel wouldn't take no for an answer. He said, "Well, I'm going to have Bruce Allen talk to you."

Allen was the Raiders' senior executive. Bruce called me up and said, "I talked to Joe Bugel and I want to talk to you."

There was a Denny's restaurant right next to my hotel. So we met there at about 10:00 p.m. And we were still there until four in the morning. Bruce wrote me out a coaching contract with the Raiders on a napkin and wanted me to sign it.

I said, "Bruce, I'm telling you for the last time, I gave Mike Ditka my word. And I'm not going to go to him and tell him my word doesn't mean anything, I'm going to New Orleans." That decision probably cost me $100,000. But that's okay.

I still have that contract on the napkin at my house in Hilton Head.

We had a lot of good players in Detroit. But it felt like we were always trying to get over the hump. I enjoyed working in

Detroit, and I enjoyed the city of Detroit. I lived out in Auburn Hills, and it was beautiful.

I liked coaching with Wayne, who lives in Tarpon Springs, just north of the Gulf beaches in Tampa Bay. I see him from time to time in Tampa. He's been one of my closest friends in coaching.

"For him to not get a head coaching job and only two interviews, I can't believe that Tom Moore was never a head coach," Fontes said. "I can't believe his demeanor, how he handled people. He was articulate, smart. He got along with the players and for him not to be a head coach, I'm amazed. I'm amazed at the National Football League that it didn't happen."

I almost returned to Detroit many years later. The Lions were one of two head-coaching jobs I interviewed for during my career. In 1984, I interviewed with the University of Minnesota, and they hired Lou Holtz. Lou had been a graduate assistant at Iowa my senior year. Then, many years later, in 2006, I interviewed for the Lions head coaching job with Matt Millen, their general manager.

They hired defensive line coach Rod Marinelli, and he deserved it. He was a good coach and deserved it.

They hired Mike Martz as offensive coordinator and fell on some rough times, losing all 16 games for the first time in NFL history.

But I told myself, "You better figure, Tom, you ain't going to get a head coaching job. So don't worry about it. Be the best assistant coach that you can be. That's your role." And that's what I've always tried to be.

It goes back to my first job in Pittsburgh. Back then, assistant coaches were to be seen and not heard. There was one voice and it belonged to Chuck Noll.

Bill Polian paid me the biggest compliment he could pay me. When I left the Colts, he wrote me a letter. And he said, "I always thought of you as my R&R coach—Results, not Recognition." That meant a lot to me.

You always want to be a head coach but there's only thirty-two jobs. There were always some things working against me. I don't have a lot of charisma. I pretty much tell things the way they are. If you don't want an answer, don't ask me a question. I really don't enjoy playing the bullshit game. I don't feel that I wasn't a success because I wasn't a head coach.

But look at the players I got to coach.

10

The Receiving Corps

Swann & Stallworth, Harrison & Wayne

HE WAS ALREADY a Super Bowl MVP and a star in the league. He was from a big school—Southern California—and had a big smile and a huge personality. He was the Steelers' first-round pick in the 1974 draft.

And he was the first guy who came to see me after I was hired as the Steelers receiving coach. Lynn Swann.

The Steelers' other starting receiver was John Stallworth, who was taken in the fourth round of the '74 draft from tiny Alabama A&M in Huntsville. Of course, I knew of him and had watched him play.

They were consummate professionals. They made each other better because one guy wanted to be better than the other.

John was a great football player when he arrived as a rookie, but the Steelers also had a receiver by the name of Frank Lewis.

Back in those days, we had a right wide receiver and left wide receiver. Frank was anchored there on the left side, and Swann on the right, so John was left playing a backup role.

After the '77 season, Pittsburgh traded Frank to Buffalo, and Stallworth took over. Both he and Swann had tremendous work ethic and tremendous pride. They pulled for each other, but also competed against each other.

They wanted to learn how to read coverages and that's what we worked on.

I had a worksheet when I coached receivers. And as I put a play in, the receivers wrote it down. That was Paul Brown. It's what he used to do.

As a receiver, you want to know where to line up in the formation. What route do you want me to run? How deep do you want me to run it? Are there any adjustments to the route? Am I involved in any kind of blitz control responsibilities? Where's my reception area? Where should I be open? As I put it in, they filled in the boxes.

That's the way we put in plays. They wrote it down. There were no iPads. The belief was that if you wrote it, you'd learn it. To play for legendary coach Paul Brown, you had to be extremely intellectual. He took smart guys.

I told Chuck Noll one time that I was going to give the quarterbacks a written test. Chuck said, "I don't care what you're doing, but Terry Bradshaw is starting."

That ended that idea.

They tell me when Paul Brown came in to Cleveland, he had the meeting room furnished with the same number of chairs as players. They had a strip of tape on each chair with the name of every player who was supposed to be there. He knew if anybody was missing when he walked into the meeting room.

I was pretty strict, too, though I adapted my ways a bit. Dungy remembered how I brought lots of rules from my college coaching days to Pittsburgh, and how those rules might not sit well with the pros.

"But he figured out what Swann and Stallworth needed. It's like Stallworth and Swann said. We can catch the ball. We needed to understand what was happening on defense in coverage and how we could adapt to things we were seeing."

Lionel Taylor was a popular Steelers receivers coach who had played the position in the NFL. Swann and Stallworth knew him well, but they weren't sure what I was all about. I had to earn their trust.

"Lionel played the game and knew a lot about being on the field, how to beat a guy in coverage," Stallworth said. "There was a lot of man coverage and Lionel taught us how to run routes and we already knew how to catch the football.

"We were doing well. I don't know how, but we realized right away there was still a void there. We were doing well. You know, Tom's voice was kind of gravelly and kind of hesitant a little bit. He came in and we hadn't heard him before. Our first impression was that this guy is scared.

"We've got a lot of questions now. We soon learned that was his natural voice. We learned there was a part of the game, a cerebral part of the game we were lacking, and Tom commenced right away to bring us up to speed on that. Once we realized that, and the sincerity in the man—he wanted to do a good job—we knew he wanted the best for us. He wanted to know us and understand us, and that brought him close to us as a group. It took a little while for us to get there but we got there, and we got very comfortable with Tom and what he added to us and the value he communicated to us."

Right about the time I came into the league, Bud Carson—who coached for the Steelers and then the Rams—for all practical purposes was the guy who introduced Cover 2.

It's named after the two deep safeties, who have a big burden and a lot of field to cover. Therefore, they must get a lot of help from the underneath coverage to keep receivers from outnumbering them in the deep zones. Bud also devised variations and compatible coverages, where every defender is responsible for an area of the field and not a specific man, that go with Cover 2 in the NFL.

We used them at Georgia Tech when I was coaching under Bud there from '71 to '72. Pretty much before Bud came to the NFL, the pro teams played a lot of Cover 1 and Cover 3 zone.

As the passing game opened up, the way it did when we couldn't use bump and run, people became more creative with disguising coverages, changing coverages up from one deep to two deep, and from one deep zone to one deep man, to two deep zone to two deep man, to man combinations where you'd trap people, double coverage on different receivers. Also, the zone blitz package became very prominent.

I don't know what was taught before I got there, and I'm certainly not critical because, before I got there, it was a different game from a passing standpoint.

What we did is we watched a lot of tape of different teams and how they were applying it. When we went to training camp, everybody was used to one-on-one, which was receivers against defensive backs. Because of the nuances of coverage, we spent half that time working on double coverage concepts and schemes where people go short and long on you, where people go in and out on you, where people would read the releases by the No. 2 receiver to determine what they were going to do and how to defend the No. 1 receiver. This corresponded with your blocking assignments. Sometimes, you blocked what we called the MDM, which stood for the Most Dangerous Man. Other times you would block support. Other times you'd block a cornerback or a strong safety. You'd have a designated guy you would block. Well, when they rotated after the snap and went to double coverages, you had to adjust and adapt to that.

I think the evolution of the receiver position was the result of the advent of Cover 2 and Two Man and all the combination coverages that stemmed from that particular scheme.

It can be attributed to Bud Carson and, of course, the fact that the NFL is a copycat league. They went to Cover 2 and now everybody calls it Tampa 2. That's a variation and that was really created by Jack Lambert at Pittsburgh. When Tony Dungy was there, Jack Lambert was the middle linebacker and on Cover 2, which is zone coverage, he'd keep dropping deep. He'd drop deeper and deeper and Tony asked him, "Why are you going so deep?" And Jack said, "Because nobody is in front of me." That became the Tampa 2. When you have a middle linebacker, you keep getting depth until somebody is in front of you, and when they are, you come up and play normal Cover 2.

There were all these variations and nuances meant to help the coverage because they'd taken away the bump and run with the Mel Blount Rule.

Because of that, we changed what we did on offense. It was no longer all one-on-one, defender against receiver. Now there was a lot of combination coverage, a lot of double coverage. For us, it was a lot of working with the receivers on 1) identifying the coverage you get when you come off the line of scrimmage, because they're going to hold it as long as they can to try and disguise it. And 2) once you recognize it coming off the line of scrimmage, you need to process the technique you need to use to get open and defeat that type of coverage.

We worked on teaching coverage concepts.

Our practices were competitive, as you would expect. In addition to competing with Lynn Swann, Stallworth always wanted to go up against Mel Blount in practice. They had a lot in common. Blount had also played for a small southern school—Southern University and A&M College in Baton Rouge.

John Stallworth was a hard worker. Mel Blount was a great defensive back. He played the right cornerback position and John Stallworth played the left wide receiver. When we would go to training camp and minicamp, when we did one-on-one drills, Stallworth only wanted to go against Mel and Mel only wanted to go against Stallworth. If another receiver lined up during Mel Blount's turn, Blount would say, "Get him out of here. I want Stallworth." If it was Stallworth's turn and somebody else lined up against him, he would say, "I want Blount."

Those were great battles. Stallworth was considered a big receiver at 6' 2", 191 pounds with long arms and legs. But Blount was even bigger at 6' 3", 205.

Once Blount got his hands on a receiver, it was over. Remember, they changed the rules in 1978 so that defensive backs were barred from contact with receivers after five yards because of Blount.

When those two went at it, it was like two battering rams.

When the ball was snapped in one-on-one drills, Stallworth was a technician as a route runner. Blount's recognition of routes was elite, and he could run it for the receiver. Each rep was full speed and they each won as many as they lost.

I would say it probably came out 50-50. But I think the biggest value of it was that with two greats going against each other, the competition only made them each better. You get a lot of coaching techniques and things, but then you have to apply them, and I think both of those guys were able to apply them against each other. Ultimately it made them Hall of Famers.

Swann and Stallworth were different receivers, each uniquely talented and driven. They were both tireless workers and they didn't want to come out of the game. Lynn Swann was 5-foot-11 and only 180 pounds. He ran well and of course had made a lot of plays at USC. He was more balletic in his movement.

Where Swann was different is that he had a knack for making the spectacular catch, the kind that gets you on television highlight reels. He played the game in the air, always leaping and diving for the football.

That same catch that Swann made look so exciting, John would just run through it and snatch it.

"We came in the first year as competitors, not knowing each other," Stallworth said. "I'm excited about coming into the NFL, I'm excited about being a Pittsburgh Steeler. But I know there's at least one guy they valued above me and that was our No. 1 draft choice. I don't know any of the veteran guys, but I know in this draft class, they thought Swann was No. 1 and I was a fourth rounder. I'm right away in a competitive mode. I got to be better than that guy. I can see that now. I don't know the veteran guys, but I got to be better than that guy.

"But the way they played us . . . we had veteran guys ahead of us: Frank Lewis and Ron Shanklin. Those guys played the first quarter of every game. Then Lynn and I played the second quarter. Those guys would play the third and we'd finish up. Now Lynn and I are a team. It was just us against the veteran guys.

"We went through that a couple years. After one year, Lewis was traded, but then Lynn gets to play, and he immediately gets a rapport with Terry. He's now got confidence in Lynn. He's taking snaps from center, and on the passing downs, he's looking right and I'm fighting for attention on the left side, so now we're competitors again fighting for Bradshaw's attention. We went through that for most of our careers.

"In hindsight, as I look through stuff, we were together for a lot of things. We have a lot of videos of the team during our time together and there are shots of us sitting together and doing things together. But we got on the field, and it was those competitive juices. I think it was healthy for our scheme that we were competitors, that we were striving to be better than the other guy. It was never that we harbored any ill will or thought 'I don't want that guy over there to catch any passes.' It was none of that.

"It was just, 'I want to be better.' If he caught four passes, I wanted to catch five. We went through that, and it was healthy for the team, but it was not healthy for our relationship. It was an edge that was always there when we got together.

"One time our receivers went out for dinner and a guy came over to our table and he was just all over me and all over Lynn. Then the guy says, 'Mr. Swann, you're great and the other guys are okay.' Lynn knows what's going on. He looks at the guy and says, 'Sir, you probably need to leave right now.'"

The two Super Bowls the Steelers won before I arrived were about running the football and playing badass defense. The two we won when I was there were about passing the football.

"What he learned is how to use all these guys," Tony Dungy said. "He's got Swann and Stallworth but also Franco and [Rocky] Bleier. In Detroit, he's got Barry Sanders and he's got to get him the ball, but he's also got Herman Moore and Brett Perriman and Johnny Morton, and they want to catch it. How do you use them?"

Coaching Swann and Stallworth was great. We started to have success. We started throwing the ball more. Terry Bradshaw was coming on and doing a great job.

No matter what Stallworth did, Swann just seemed to get a little more attention. I have one funny story, and John's the one who told me. It was around Christmas, and he was around South Hills Village in the mall with his son. I'm not sure the age of his son at that time. He was probably like five or six years old. Very impressionable. This was after Lynn Swann had retired. So some lady came up and recognized John and introduced herself. She was just being friendly. She asked John's son, "Who's your favorite receiver?" The little boy looked up and without batting an eye said, with his father standing there, "Lynn Swann." John told me, "I wanted to grab him!" But everything was in good nature. They had such tremendous respect for each other.

Terry Bradshaw looked at Swann and Stallworth as equal receivers.

"Stallworth was just as good," Bradshaw said. "He wasn't as flamboyant as Lynn was. But they were both Hall of Famers."

However, Bradshaw said he had more in common with Stallworth.

"John went to a historically Black college in Alabama and Lynn went to USC in Los Angeles," Bradshaw said. "I felt more in touch with John because I went to a small school in the South. He went to a small school in the South. Lynn came in and was already extremely polished. A first-round pick. He was very mature, and it took me a while to even halfway grow up.

"Lynn was so supremely confident in what he was doing, and John knew he had to excel on the field because he went to Alabama A&M. He had to compete to prove he was better. Lynn very seldom complained. John would every now and then. He would come over and say, 'Hey, Brad, what did I do? I do business.' And I would say, 'Yeah, I got it.' And if they pissed me off, I wouldn't throw it to them. I could easily flip the play from one side to the other."

In 1977, the year I joined the Steelers, we also drafted Jim Smith, who was a really good receiver from Michigan. He was a big guy, 6-foot-2, 205 pounds. As I said earlier, Chuck wanted to find a way to get him on the field, as well.

"Jimmy Smith was funny," Bradshaw said. "He'd come in talking tough and talking trash. I just loved him and I'm still close with him today. He came to me when he was young. But he'd say, 'Are you going to throw me the fucking ball or what? You always ignore my ass.' He was a stud. I hit him in Chicago for about three touchdown passes one game. He liked that."

Both Swann and Stallworth were very good students. They learned quickly.

"He spent a lot of time on the board, talking about coverages," Stallworth said. "We knew how to beat a guy, but Tom was about the numbers—exactly how to do that.

"It was more predicated on the coverage and what that guy was supposed to do. He taught us what the assignment of that corner was in that coverage. So if you're attacking here and he's doing what he's supposed to do, this is the way you can beat him. It added some simplicity to the game. Whatever the coverage was, we knew how to consistently beat it. We spent a lot of time on the board and less time on the field because Tom was playing to his strong suit, and that's teaching. He wasn't going to get out there and show us how to run a route.

"Tom's role with the team kind of grew. He came in as the receivers coach and he brought a lot of knowledge with him. Our last few years, he grew from our receivers coach to our offensive coordinator. We saw him grow in a very short time frame from the time he came in to playing a heavy role and doing things that an offensive coordinator does but just not having it attached to his name. We saw him grow as we approached those last two Super Bowls."

As I mentioned, Swann was always on the right side and Stallworth on the left. When you do that, you get twice as much work because you're not going all over the place.

That was Chuck Noll's philosophy and it worked for him, and it worked for me.

We did the same thing in Indianapolis with Marvin Harrison and Reggie Wayne two decades later.

Marvin was already with the Colts when we got there. He was a guy who was as hard of a worker as you could imagine. He fits right in there with the Barry Sanderses, the Swanns, the Stallworths, the Franco Harrises.

He was just relentless. He wanted to take every snap, and so did Reggie. The big question the Colts faced going into the 2001 draft was do you take Reggie Wayne or Santana Moss? Well, Bill Polian and his expertise believed you go big and fast over small and fast. It proved to be true. Santana had some injury problems—hamstring pulls and things like that—but Reggie didn't.

Marvin taught Reggie how to be a professional with his work ethic. Again, I go back to what we did in Pittsburgh. We did it in Indianapolis. We had a right wide receiver and a left wide receiver. I keep bringing it up and that's what I believe in.

They both competed. The thing about Marvin and Reggie, you see all the substitution packages going in these days? That wouldn't fly with them. I used to tell Lynn and John and Reggie and Marvin, "Hey, you want to come out of the game, or do you want to score a touchdown?" But this in and out, back and forth and all that stuff. They stayed in and took every snap. Even if you wanted to take them out of the game, oh man, you'd have an argument because they ain't coming out. They're going to play the game and they're going to get a feel for the game.

The year Marvin caught 143 passes, some newspaper reporter asked him if he knew how many passes he'd caught. This was late in the season. He said, "I don't worry about how many passes I've caught. You guys count them, I'll catch them." That's the way all four of them were. They wanted every football thrown to them. They were always open. But they also appreciated and respected the other guy and pulled for him.

In the grand scheme of things, they wanted to win. Whatever it takes to win. Because, ultimately, that's what you're judged on.

"It didn't make sense to most people at first," Dungy said.

Always putting the same receivers on the same side of the formation would seem to make it easier for the opponent to set their defense.

"He did it with Swann and Stallworth and we were doing it twenty years later [at Indianapolis with Marvin Harrison and Reggie Wayne]," Dungy said. "But now there's all these wacky formations teams are using and, yeah, they might be good. But this still works, too.

"The other thing is Peyton Manning wanted to see the whole defense and see what they're in. He looked for body language and all that. We're going to line up quick, get out there fast so he had longer to look at the defense."

As a play caller, I didn't script the first fifteen plays. I scripted openers—the start of a series. The reason was because what I did on second down would depend on what happened on first down. And what I did on third down depended on what we did on second down.

I never wanted to be a hostage to the call sheet. I had an inventory of plays for certain coverages. What's my best pass if I start seeing three-deep zone? If I'm in a 3 x 1 formation, some people will slide to zone strong side and then play man-to-man weak side. People want to throw strong. If they take that away, what's my answer to Cover 2? What's my answer to Two Man? If they're rushing two or rushing three and dropping, what do we do?

First of all, I insisted that nobody was going to sack the quarterback. You had to have the right protections. That was the most important part of my call sheet.

I basically had the game plan and play sheet memorized before each game. I called plays collectively for almost forty years in my coaching career. When you call plays, you got roughly sixty-five of them in any given game. As Chuck Noll told me one time, after the event, even a fool is wise. I think Shakespeare said that one time.

You have sixty-five decisions to make in each game and ten seconds to make each one. Have a plan, work the plan, and believe in your plan. When you get a quarterback like Peyton Manning, you can give him the opportunity to change it.

COACHING POINTS

FIVE FOOTBALL ESSENTIALS

▶ **CDC: Choices, Decisions, and Consequences**

That's life. That's how life is.

The other thing that was important to me was field position. Were we backed up inside our 10-yard line? I highlighted plays for that. Once we cross midfield, I had plays I liked on that spot on the field. Then on third down, what am I thinking third and 2 to 7? And what am I thinking third and 8-plus?

I hated going to the Monday morning meetings saying, "Damn!"

Here's how I practiced memorizing the game plan. On Saturday, I always got to my room in the team hotel and I'd watch two college games. I'd watch the one o'clock game and the four o'clock game. When we were on the road, I would just catch the four o'clock game. Say I'm watching Iowa play Northwestern. I would take my call sheet and pretend I was the play-caller for Iowa. I go through my script based on situations that exist in that game I'm watching on TV. I use our game plan. You get real live situations. You're watching the game, and the guy lost the ball at the 1-yard line, what are you going to call? Right now.

I'm just explaining how I did it. But, believe me, there are a million ways to skin a cat.

TODAY, YOU HAVE a 17-game regular-season schedule. You've got to take the first game like it's the Super Bowl and hope the last game *is* the Super Bowl. To maintain that, you've got to be steady.

The first Super Bowl the Steelers played in was Super Bowl IX and they beat the Vikings 16–6. The score at halftime was 2–0 with the Purple People Eaters against the Steel Curtain. Fran Tarkenton was chased all over the field by the Steel Curtain and threw 3 interceptions.

Joe Greene shut down the Vikings run game, which gained only 17 yards on 21 attempts.

Bradshaw needed only 9 pass completions to get the job done.

The next year, they played in Super Bowl X against the Dallas Cowboys and beat them 21–17.

Swann caught 4 passes for 161 yards and a TD to become the first receiver to be named the MVP of the Super Bowl.

I got there when we went to Super Bowl XIII against Dallas and we had 66 yards rushing and 291 yards passing. In Super Bowl XIV against the Rams, we had 309 yards passing and 84 yards rushing.

"They changed the rules on pass defense, and we tried to do some of the West Coast Offense and I wasn't used to dealing with it," Bradshaw said. "Our primary way of throwing the football was to go down the field.

"Tom was always so encouraging. He'd say, 'Don't worry about it, just keep throwing that ball down there!'"

Terry was smart and he called his own plays. We'd go over the game plan, but he would make the changes based on what he was seeing.

"The great thing about calling your own plays, you get in the huddle, and you have a play and you can say, 'We can't do it, they're in the three technique,' or whatever," Bradshaw said. "So you say, 'How about this? Yeah, let's do that.' See, I could do that in the huddle.

"I said to Lynn, 'Don't run the post in.' He said, 'What do you want?' I said, 'How about a post corner option to either one?' Or sometimes *he* would say that. That was the great thing about calling your own plays. I don't know if I could've done it today because of all the formations. But there's still only five guys who can go out and catch the ball."

We had two plays against the Dallas Cowboys that won us the game. Two plays. They came up with both linebackers inside. We called it Double Barrel. We always had a tight end, so we saw it. We had a tackle trap where the guards blocked out, the center blocked one way, the tackle trapped the other guy. We ran the tackle trap. Franco went 22 yards for a touchdown.

Then they came up again, and Franco stepped up to block. We're going to throw the ball. They rush, Franco blocks the guy and releases, and Bradshaw throws it to him for another 22-yard gain. You take advantage of what people do. The next year we played the Rams in the Super Bowl out there in the Rose Bowl. We had two backs and we had a split end and flanker in the slot. Three of the Rams assistant coaches had previously been at Pittsburgh—receivers coach Lionel Taylor, offensive line coach Dan Radakovich, and defensive coordinator Bud Carson.

They knew everything about the Steelers, and if you don't believe it, ask them. But we knew what Bud would do on third down. He's going to go prevent and we'd get flanker, slot, split end. Bud was going to go into the nickel defense. He was going to prevent. He was going to go man to man on the flanker. He was going to go short and long on the split end, and he was going to go in and out on the slot.

Swann had gotten hurt. But not before he caught a 47-yard TD pass from Bradshaw to give us a 17–13 lead. They knocked

Swann out of the game with a concussion. So that meant he was replaced by Theo Bell. The flanker was going to play man-to-man. That was Jim Smith. For the slot, that was Stallworth—he was going to go in and out, kind of a bracket coverage. So what we did is, we ran those on flag routes, and we took Stallworth and brought him down and he ran a 12-yard in, post. Because when you run an in-route, the inside guy jumps in, the outside guy laps over, so you're running and in-post, not an in-takeoff.

We knew he was going to be in that coverage. Sixty prevent, Slot Hook and Go. Stallworth ran by the Rams' Rod Perry. The ball was thrown over his outside shoulder and Stallworth made the adjustment to catch it. The play went for a 73-yard touchdown. Then Stallworth got another big gainer (45 yards) on the same play and Franco scored. Those were two key touchdowns to win the game.

After we won Super Bowl XIII, Chuck Noll said, "I don't believe we've peaked yet." As usual, he was right.

That's why it was so great working for Chuck Noll. Because whether it was real or not, when you worked and played for Chuck Noll, you always knew there would never be a tie game because you had Chuck. He'd be the difference. Without those two plays against Dallas, we don't beat them. Without those two plays against the Rams—the Rams were a damn good team that year—we don't beat them.

Vince Ferragamo, the Rams quarterback, got hot that year. But he was throwing a crossing route that Jack Lambert intercepted. That was the turning point in the game.

Not surprisingly, Terry Bradshaw was the MVP of those last two games against the Cowboys and Rams.

I've been blessed with great players, especially receivers, almost everywhere I've coached.

At Minnesota, of course, I got to coach Anthony Carter. When he was at Michigan, Bo Schembechler came out and made a bold statement. Bo was very run-oriented because of his training from Woody Hayes, who thought the only thing that happens when you pass the ball is an interception or incompletion. Bo said Anthony Carter changed his whole perspective on the passing game. He was that great.

Cris Carter (not related to Anthony) turned out to be phenomenal. I don't know if I mentioned how the Vikings actually got Cris Carter. I think it was the last cut and a player by the name of Leo Lewis, who was a veteran, we were going to slip through the waiver wire because we didn't think anybody would pick him up. Then, once he cleared waivers, we were going to bring him back. Sure enough, Cleveland claimed Lewis off waivers and now we've got a spot open on the roster. About the same time, Philadelphia shockingly cut Cris Carter. We got Cris, and a week later, the Browns cut Leo Lewis, so we signed him back. By cutting Leo, we ended up getting Cris Carter.

Cris Carter's brother, Butch, had been the captain of the basketball team at Indiana under coach Bob Knight. This was while Cris was a great athlete in both football and basketball in high school in Middleton, Ohio. He was being recruited for hoops, as well. Coach Knight called his home one night, and his mother answered. He wanted to know if he was going to go to Indiana or play football. Her other son was a captain, after all, and Cris had attended the basketball camps at Indiana.

Cris was undecided. His mother told the Indiana legend, "Coach Knight, I know you, and I know Cris, and you don't want this one. I think he's going to play football." So he ended up going to Ohio State and was a phenomenal football player there. When he came to the Vikings, Cris Carter and I became tight. He was a good, good person. He just needed a little guidance, so I spent a lot of time with him.

Of course, he went on to have an unbelievable career with the Vikings. He was an unbelievably hard worker. And so was Jake Reed, who overcame an eye issue with the Vikings to become one of the more productive receivers in the league. Of all the great receivers I've worked with—Swann, Stallworth, Marvin Harrison, and Reggie Wayne—the great ones, their work ethic was out of sight. Nobody could match them.

Like Swann and Stallworth, Harrison and Wayne wanted to catch every pass. But they wanted to win more than anything else and were willing to do what it takes.

In the AFC Championship Game when we came back from a 21–3 deficit to beat the Patriots and go to the Super Bowl, we got a 1-yard touchdown reception from defensive tackle / fullback Dan Klecko and a huge 32-yard reception from tight end Bryan Fletcher.

"The last two drives, we had Marvin Harrison, Dallas Clark in the slot, Bryan Fletcher at tight end, and Reggie Wayne," Dungy said. "Bill Belichick's whole thing was, Marvin Harrison was not going to beat us. Put the best guy on Reggie Wayne and live with the rest. Peyton and Bryan Fletcher came up with this play they'd never run. Okay, here's the coverage, this is what they're doing. We're going to go to the corner. How can we design this so you go to the corner and everybody else gets out? And they're doing it on the fly. It was a 32-yard play. A play we had never run before. It set up Joseph Addai's touchdown. That's the beauty of Tom's system. What does it take? Okay, we've got

TOM MOORE

this route in. We haven't done it this way, but it's the answer to this coverage we haven't seen."

Coming to Tampa Bay, I knew wide receiver Mike Evans was a future Hall of Fame player. He's proven that with the work and the production he had put in over the years. He just completed his tenth straight season with at least 1,000 yards receiving while tying for the NFL lead with 13 touchdowns. Another receiver I think is tremendous is Chris Godwin. He works hard, studies hard, and practices hard. He does everything with great precision and perfection. He never says anything negative. He's the consummate professional football player.

Lynn Swann waited a long time to be elected to the Pro Football Hall of Fame. When Swann finally got the call that he was in as part of the 2001 class, Stallworth had been a finalist seven times and still had not received enough votes to be inducted. Stallworth had also played longer. He lasted 14 seasons to Swann's 9 and caught 22 more passes for 3,300 more yards than his teammate.

They wanted to be the best. I think the greatest testimony for their feelings for each other was when Lynn was inducted into the Pro Football Hall of Fame before John went in. In part of his speech during the induction ceremony, this is what he said:

COACHING POINTS

THINGS YOU HAVE TO GUARD AGAINST

▶ **Systems**

Liam Coen, whose time as offensive coordinator with the Bucs overlapped with my ongoing role with the team, has got a great system. He knows its problems, he knows how to solve them. But it's still people. It's still about the players.

I've been to five Super Bowls with three different systems and we won because it was the people. People win.

"If this is the greatest hour of my life, then I will tell you at this moment, this is only a half hour," Swann said. "It will be the greatest hour when I can sit in that back row and John Stallworth is wearing a gold jacket and making this speech."

The very next year, John Stallworth was enshrined into the Pro Football Hall of Fame. They're together again in Canton, Ohio.

11

Jake Reed and the Vikings

YOU WANT TO KNOW what an assistant coach does that you never hear about?

Let me tell you about my time with the Vikings, when in 1991 we drafted a receiver from Grambling State in the third round. Jake Reed.

He was big—6-foot-3, 213 pounds. He was fast. But Reed had one problem when he got to training camp—he kept dropping the football.

Denny Green came to the Vikings as head coach a year later, and he wanted to get rid of Jake because he was struggling so badly catching the football.

"In practice, when I would line up to the left of the quarterback, my depth perception was off," Reed said. "I kept dropping the ball and the ball would get up on me. If I was on the right side of the quarterback, I was catching everything. I was catching all the slants and everything. On the left side, I just had a problem and Tom recognized it. He said, 'Something is going on with his eye.'"

We didn't figure this out right away. Before the discovery, Reed had trouble adjusting to the NFL.

Part of the problem was that we were loaded at receiver with the Vikings. We had Cris Carter, Anthony Carter, Hassan Jones, and Leo Lewis. Reed was having a hard time finding his role.

Reed said, "Tom was one of those guys who walked around and had that gravelly voice. 'Hey, Jake! What the hell are you doing?' he'd say. And I knew I wasn't going to play as a rookie. I knew I wasn't going to be on the practice squad because I was a third-round pick. So I'd practice during the week, and on game day I would be in my street clothes. I was inactive all year long. I can remember a time when Cris Carter would have a bad game, and Tom would curse *me* out. 'Dammit, Jake! Why'd you run the wrong route?' I'm like, 'I don't know, Tom. I'm on the sideline with you.'

"'Quit running the wrong routes!' He would get on me so bad in practice. If I ran a bad play—I was young and trying to learn the offense—he would yell at me, 'Did you run the wrong route again? I'm going to get your ass out of here!'

"I'm thinking, man, this guy is always cursing me out. He's always on me. Here was this older white guy on me and I wasn't used to that. I said, 'We ain't going to make it.' I was talking to Cris Carter and Anthony Carter and being all bad with them. They said, 'Boy, you need to go talk to Tom.' I said, 'I can't let him talk to me like that.'

"I walked up to Tom, and he said, 'What the hell do you want, Jake? You had a pretty good practice but you're still dropping too many balls and you're forgetting stuff.' I said, 'I need to talk to you. Why do you keep getting on me so hard?'

I said, 'When Cris Carter and them drop a ball, you're on me. Anthony Carter has a bad play, you're on me. I just need to know.'

"He grabbed me by the wrist and said, 'Let me tell you something right now. When I stop hollering at your ass, and stop getting on you, you're going to be on the first bus out of here!'

"I said, 'Okay. We're cool, Tom.'

"But when Tom made that statement, my whole attitude changed. I said, 'He sees something in me that I don't see.' After that, I prepared differently. I approached practice differently, and I just started getting better. Our relationship changed. I realized his getting on me and pushing me wasn't in a negative way. It wasn't because he didn't like me. He saw something in me."

Jerry Reichow was the Vikings director of football operations. I had recruited his son, Alan, to the University of Minnesota but he didn't come. He was now Dr. Alan Reichow, Nike's Global Research Director for Vision Sciences. At Nike, he applied sound vision science principles to improve performance.

I flew out to Portland and met with Alan. I looked at all the apparatuses that he had for tests. And he'd had success with a couple baseball players. He showed me the tests. I said, "Well, we've got Jake Reed and he has a problem. He's a great athlete but he's having trouble catching the ball."

Dr. Reichow said, "Don't tell me what the problems are but send him out here. You know what they are; I don't want to know. Send him out here and we'll do these tests," and he did. Then he sent me a synopsis with what he found. He was right on the button with everything.

Jake Reed wasn't sold right away. He was young and talented. How could vision be his problem?

"I thought he was kind of crazy for a minute," Reed said. "We had that conversation, then in the offseason, he said, 'You're going to Portland to get your eyes fixed.'"

Our training staff and the conditioning guys weren't really sold on this. The guy who really got it going was Paul Wiggin. He was the Vikings' senior consultant for pro personnel, and he took charge and said, "We're going to get it done."

When something comes at your eyes, your pupils narrow for focus. With Jake, the ball was on him before his eyes could focus. He particularly had trouble focusing with his right eye when he lined up on the left side.

I said, "Okay, now that we know the problems, what do we do?" Dr. Reichow had an intern in Minneapolis that was an optometrist and Jake had me as a coach. So for two offseasons, we worked every morning five days a week, for two or two and a half hours, on different ball-catching drills. All to train his eyes.

Dr. Reichow told me which routes Jake would have trouble with, so I told him we'd run those repeatedly and I'd throw it to him.

We'd meet in the mornings, and I took a volleyball and sat a couple feet away and I'd bounce it to him and he'd catch it. Bounce. Catch. Bounce. Catch.

Then, we went smaller. I got it down to a softball because we were working on focusing. Then I dropped a tennis ball and he caught it, because it was even smaller. Then I took a Ping-Pong ball and that's it. Ever try to catch a Ping-Pong ball with two hands? It's not easy.

Then we'd go to a racquetball court. I got a strobe light, like when you go to nightclubs, and I'd throw a football to him. As the week went along, the light got shorter and shorter. He'd have to come out of being in the dark for longer periods with just a little light and have to focus to find the ball.

We did those in the offseason every day for the two years I was there. I did my thing in the morning and in the afternoon Jake went to the optometrist and did different things for his vision. Jake spent about four or five hours a day for two years working on this.

"That was the most draining time," Jake said. "I would be more tired doing that than if I practiced. With your eyes focusing that long, and putting red and green glasses on, working on eye movement. I'm standing on one of those balance balls and have to keep your balance and reach out and catch the ball. It was like two hours. We spent the whole offseason doing that over and over. With my right hand. With my left hand. The left eye, the right eye. With a patch over my left eye and then I just had to focus. They did a little bit on my good eye, just trying to balance it out.

"Tom and I really became good friends. Great friends. I think it was a situation where Tom saw a lot in me that I didn't see in myself, and he pushed me to be great.

"I didn't really want to accept it, but as I got going, I understood that he knew what he was talking about. . . . He made me stay up there during the offseason. I didn't really like that. But the following year, I started catching everything."

It paid off for Jake Reed and the Vikings.

Jake had an outstanding career. He went on to have four 1,000-yard seasons. He played 12 seasons for the Vikings and Saints. He finished with 450 career receptions for 6,999 yards and 36 touchdowns.

He also did it playing with a lot of different quarterbacks: Sean Salisbury, Jim McMahon, Jeff George, Warren Moon, Randall Cunningham, and Brad Johnson.

"Coming in as a young guy, I got drafted and I had some money and I thought I had made it," Jake said. "But there was a lot more than just making it. Tom wanted me to be great. And I think I would've had 10,000 yards if Tom Moore had stayed with the Vikings.

"I still worked at it, but I didn't work as hard on my eye discipline as I did with Tom because Tom was on me. I had respect for him. If he said, 'Be here at seven o'clock in the morning,' I would be there at six forty-five. I could not be late because Tom was not going to tolerate that.

"He didn't care if you had started, or you had six 1,000-yard seasons. 'This is what you're doing. This is how you're going to do it.' I took that to heart because I knew how much he cared. It's almost like a kid trying to please their parents. You did not want to disappoint them. I think I had gotten to that stage with Tom working with me. I did not want to disappoint him because Tom put all the work in with me.

"Today, these kids want everything fast. I don't think he could get someone to sit down and do all that. They're making so much money now, they'll tell you they don't need it. I'm telling you, I sucked it all in and it's been a wonderful thing for my life."

Denny was good to me. He brought in Jack Burns as the offensive coordinator. He'd been with the Redskins, and they had just won the Super Bowl. After the second game of that second year, Dennis let Jack Burns go and made Brian Billick the offensive coordinator. So Brian takes over and it's obvious to me that Brian may want his own receivers coach.

We're at a staff meeting and Denny was telling us what his goal was for the Vikings, which was to win a Super Bowl. He wanted to get the Vikings into the position that San Francisco was in, because he'd coached for the 49ers. He coached for Bill

Walsh and was part of those great teams they had in the '80s. He was telling us he wanted to get the Vikings to be like the 49ers where nobody wanted to play them because people were afraid of them.

It kind of rang a bell with me because during my time with the Steelers in the '80s, we'd played San Francisco in 1984. We played them at Candlestick Park, and we were fortunate to beat them. In fact, they went 15–1 that season and that was their only loss. We went on to lose the AFC Championship Game to Miami. So when I heard Denny reference those Niners, it rang a bell. I stopped in Denny's office a few minutes later and said, "Hey, Denny, have you got a minute?" He said, "Yes." I said, "No offense, but when I was in Pittsburgh, trust me, we didn't fear the 49ers." He looked at me and smiled before he said, "Tom, I respect your loyalty and thank you."

The season went by, and we played the Steelers early in the season. Bill Cowher, who I have the greatest amount of respect for, was the head coach. He did a fabulous job in Pittsburgh, getting the Steelers back to the top and getting them to the Super Bowl. We go to Pittsburgh and this is Bill Cowher's first year with the Steelers and Denny's first year with the Vikings. We beat them.

At the end of the year, they named Bill Cowher Coach of the Year. I thought that was kind of strange. Sid Hartman, the longtime columnist for the *Minneapolis Star Tribune*, had been a friend since my days coaching at the University of Minnesota. We were talking one day, and I said, "You know, Sid, I don't understand how Cowher won Coach of the Year over Denny Green. We had the same record. We both were 11–5 that year. We both won our divisions. When we played head-to-head, Denny beat them, but Bill Cowher was named Coach of the Year."

I thought it was a casual conversation, but you know Sid—anytime you compliment anyone or say anything, Sid is going to put it in the newspaper. So the next day in the *Star Tribune*, the story said, "Tom Moore says Bill Cowher shouldn't have gotten Coach of the Year over Denny Green." He wrote further about it. It just so happened that the particular day that story came out, Dan Rooney was in town for some kind of league meeting. He read the story. Needless to say, he didn't take too kindly to it. The business manager back in Pittsburgh, a guy by the name of Jim Boston, who I was good friends with, called me and said, "Well, Tom, I see you shot your mouth off again." I said, "What are you talking about?" He told me about Sid's column and said, "That ain't right." I was sitting in my office wondering how to handle this, and Denny Green walked by the office. He stops in and says, "Tom, I appreciate your loyalty." And he walked out.

I went from Denny respecting my loyalty to the Steelers to Denny appreciating my loyalty to him. He was a great guy to work for.

Loyalty. As far as player–coach loyalty goes, I will forever be proud of the way Jake Reed and I devoted our time together to make him the terrific receiver he was. Reed worked his ass off, and he was able to have a nice, long, productive career. I'm thankful we were able to meet Dr. Reichow and get Jake's vision corrected.

"My eyesight improved so much that when a fly rolled by, I could see the wings on the fly," Reed said. "And Tom spent a lot of time with me, and I will forever be grateful for it. And whenever we see each other, he always gives me the biggest hug. We're good old friends.

It didn't matter how much Tom hollered at me if I was right or if I was wrong, because he cared enough to want me to do it right. You know? He wanted me to know how to get better if I did something right. There was never any back-and-forth. Some players may go off on a coach. I never did that with Tom because I understood what he was trying to do.

"I've told my wife and my son, 'If it wasn't for this guy, Tom Moore, right here, you would not be living the way you're living right now.' He really showed me what to do.

"Who would know, when you're a professional athlete, when you get to the next level, that the thing holding you back was an eye problem?"

When I was writing this book, Jake Reed probably paid me one of the greatest compliments.

"I put Tom Moore right up there with Coach Eddie Robinson," he said. "I had a lot of great coaches. I've got Coach Eddie Robinson, Tom Moore, and Denny Green. Coach Robinson taught me a lot of things as a young man. He taught me a lot about self-preservation. Tom Moore taught me it's the little things that matter when you want to play at this next level. It's not how big you are. It's not how fast you are. You have to train the little things if you want to be great."

MY COACHING CAREER

▷ 2023 Recipient of the Pro Football Hall of Fame Award of Excellence

YEAR	TEAM	ROLE	REGULAR SEASON RECORD	PLAYOFFS
2024	Tampa Bay Buccaneers	Senior Offensive Assistant Coach	TBD	TBD
2023	Tampa Bay Buccaneers	Senior Offensive Assistant Coach	9–8–0	1–1
2022	Tampa Bay Buccaneers	Senior Offensive Assistant Coach	8–9–0	0–1
2021	Tampa Bay Buccaneers	Senior Offensive Assistant Coach	13–4–0	1–1
2020	Tampa Bay Buccaneers	Senior Offensive Assistant Coach	11–5–0	4–0

YEAR	TEAM	ROLE	REGULAR SEASON RECORD	PLAYOFFS
2019	Tampa Bay Buccaneers	Senior Offensive Assistant Coach	7–9–0	0–0
2017	Arizona Cardinals	Assistant Head Coach—Offense	8–8–0	0–0
2016	Arizona Cardinals	Assistant Head Coach—Offense	7–8–1	0–0
2015	Arizona Cardinals	Assistant Head Coach—Offense	13–3–0	1–1
2014	Arizona Cardinals	Assistant Head Coach—Offense	11–5–0	0–1
2013	Arizona Cardinals	Assistant Head Coach—Offense	10–6–0	0–0
2012	Tennessee Titans	Offensive Consultant	6–10–0	0–0
2011	New York Jets	Offensive Consultant	8–8–0	0–0
2010	Indianapolis Colts	Senior Offensive Assistant Coach	10–6–0	0–1
2009	Indianapolis Colts	Offensive Coordinator	14–2–0	2–1
2008	Indianapolis Colts	Offensive Coordinator	12–4–0	0–1
2007	Indianapolis Colts	Offensive Coordinator	13–3–0	0–1
2006	Indianapolis Colts	Offensive Coordinator	12–4–0	4–0

YEAR	TEAM	ROLE	REGULAR SEASON RECORD	PLAYOFFS
2005	Indianapolis Colts	Offensive Coordinator	14–2–0	0–1
2004	Indianapolis Colts	Offensive Coordinator	12–4–0	1–1
2003	Indianapolis Colts	Offensive Coordinator	12–4–0	2–1
2002	Indianapolis Colts	Offensive Coordinator	10–6–0	0–1
2001	Indianapolis Colts	Offensive Coordinator	6–10–0	0–0
2000	Indianapolis Colts	Offensive Coordinator	10–6–0	0–1
1999	Indianapolis Colts	Offensive Coordinator	13–3–0	0–1
1998	Indianapolis Colts	Offensive Coordinator	3–13–0	0–0
1997	New Orleans Saints	Running Backs Coach	6–10–0	0–0
1996	Detroit Lions	Offensive Coordinator	5–11–0	0–0
1995	Detroit Lions	Offensive Coordinator	10–6–0	0–1
1994	Detroit Lions	Quarterbacks Coach	9–7–0	0–1
1993	Minnesota Vikings	Wide Receivers Coach	9–7–0	0–1

YEAR	TEAM	ROLE	REGULAR SEASON RECORD	PLAYOFFS
1992	Minnesota Vikings	Wide Receivers Coach	11–5–0	0–1
1991	Minnesota Vikings	Assistant Head Coach / Offensive Coordinator	8–8–0	0–0
1990	Minnesota Vikings	Assistant Head Coach / Quarterbacks Coach	6–10–0	0–0
1989	Pittsburgh Steelers	Offensive Coordinator / Quarterbacks Coach	9–7–0	1–1
1988	Pittsburgh Steelers	Offensive Coordinator / Quarterbacks Coach	5–11–0	0–0
1987	Pittsburgh Steelers	Offensive Coordinator / Quarterbacks Coach	8–7–0	0–0
1986	Pittsburgh Steelers	Offensive Coordinator / Quarterbacks Coach	6–10–0	0–0
1985	Pittsburgh Steelers	Offensive Coordinator / Quarterbacks Coach	7–9–0	0–0

YEAR	TEAM	ROLE	REGULAR SEASON RECORD	PLAYOFFS
1984	Pittsburgh Steelers	Offensive Coordinator / Quarterbacks Coach	9–7–0	1–1
1983	Pittsburgh Steelers	Offensive Coordinator	10–6–0	0–1
1982	Pittsburgh Steelers	Wide Receivers Coach	6–3–0	0–1
1981	Pittsburgh Steelers	Wide Receivers Coach	8–8–0	0–0
1980	Pittsburgh Steelers	Wide Receivers Coach	9–7–0	0–0
1979	Pittsburgh Steelers	Wide Receivers Coach	12–4–0	3–0
1978	Pittsburgh Steelers	Wide Receivers Coach	14–2–0	3–0
1977	Pittsburgh Steelers	Wide Receivers Coach	9–5 0	0–1

▶ **Years as a coordinator:** 22

▶ Called plays for 23 seasons in the NFL, 13 seasons in college football, and 2 years in the Army for a total of 38 play-calling years.

▶ **Super Bowls won:** 1978, 1979, 2006, and 2020

▶ **Conference Championships won:** 1978, 1979, 2006, 2009, and 2020

▶ **Career NFL playoff record:** 24–24.

▶ **Pre-NFL Coaching Career**
University of Minnesota (1975–1976)
Offensive coordinator, backfield

New York Stars—World Football League (1974)
Offensive coordinator

University of Minnesota (1972–1973)
Backfield coach

Georgia Tech (1970–1971)
Backfield coach

Wake Forest University (1969)
Offensive coordinator

University of Dayton (1965–1968)
Backfield coach

University of Iowa (1961–1962)
Graduate assistant, Freshman team head coach

▶ **Military Service:** Stationed in Korea and Fort Benning, Georgia (1962–1964)
First Calvary Division football coach, Fort Benning football coach

▶ **College Playing Career**
University of Iowa, Varsity (1959–1960)
Quarterback, placekicker

ACKNOWLEDGMENTS

THE REASON FOR THIS BOOK is to share all the lessons that I've learned through coaching and living a dream.

The first thing I want to do is thank my parents. They gave me life. I want to thank my brother for saving my life. He's the guy that saw me fall in a well when I was five and got somebody to get me out so I didn't drown.

I mention in one conversation with my parents, it really took me eighty-five years and writing this book to realize how great they were, how important and loving they were and all the lessons that I learned from them going through life that they taught me. None of that is appreciated when you're young.

If I had one wish in life, it would be that I could spend one hour with my parents and thank them and tell them how much I appreciate them. Sometimes, you don't get that opportunity. For anybody who is reading this book, who has parents, make sure you tell them that you love them and thank them because it's a tough job being a parent.

The original subtitle of this book was *Making the Best Better.* That's always been my goal in life, to have an opportunity to make the best better. I've had an opportunity to work with a lot of great players. I hope somewhere along the line, I've done something to help them be better. I know one thing: I thank them and I appreciate them because they certainly made me better as a coach and as a person, and that's a two-way street.

I also want to thank the NFL because, as I mentioned previously, it was a privilege to coach in the NFL. To have all the good fortune I've had and all the opportunities that I've had, you don't do that by yourself. There are a lot of people involved.

I spent thirteen years with the Steelers and thirteen years with the Colts, and I owe so much to the Rooney family and to Colts owner Jim Irsay and general manager Bill Polian.

I want to thank all those players. I want to thank all the head coaches that I've worked for and all the assistants I've coached with that helped me live this dream.

One coach I want to mention is Jim Mora. He gave me a chance to come to Indianapolis and be the Colts' offensive coordinator. Jim is a great head coach. I often feel bad because I think Jim felt that I was responsible in some way for him not being retained because of my close association with Tony Dungy. There's nothing further from the truth.

I had nothing to do with Tony Dungy being hired to replace Jim Mora. I just want to give a special thanks to Jim and to let him know that I truly appreciate him and just hope I can resolve any feelings, because I truly respect Jim as a head coach, and I hope he has the same feeling for me as his assistant.

The head coaches—Chuck Noll, Wayne Fontes, Jerry Burns, Tony Dungy, and Bruce Arians. I'm seventy years old and Bruce Arians gives me a job. Other people would not have done that, but he did, and I appreciate that.

I want to thank all the players. God knows I've been associated with a lot of great ones and it's tough to individualize them. I go way back to Lynn Swann, John Stallworth, and Terry Bradshaw. They were great players, and they took me and made me feel welcomed. I appreciate that. Throughout my whole career, and when I got to Indianapolis, the Peyton Mannings, the Marvin Harrisons, the Reggie Waynes, the Dallas Clarks, the Edgerrin Jameses, the Joseph Addais, and all these great players I've been associated with, it's been a tremendous ride.

I want to thank the assistant coaches I've been involved with. Dick Hoak was like a father to me when I went to Pittsburgh. He played in the league for ten years and coached in the league. But Dick helped me, and without him, this dream would probably have never come true. It probably wouldn't have happened, but he mentored me; he was good to me. Of course, I want to thank George Perles for getting me the job in Pittsburgh, which allowed me to coach in this league.

There are too many people to name when I think of everybody I worked with, but they know who they are, and they know I appreciate them and respect them and want to thank them.

Then I get to Tampa Bay. Wow. What a great organization. What a great place to coach. I can't thank the Glazer family enough. They've been so tremendous to me. Brian Ford, the Bucs' chief operating officer, has been so tremendous to me. The whole support staff has been so great to me.

I have so much respect and appreciation for Todd Bowles and I'm so indebted to him. Todd Bowles has done a great job. He took the head coaching job in Tampa Bay under some very hard circumstances. He had to make some tough decisions. But Todd has done a fantastic job.

In 2023, he took a team that was struggling at one point, and it was his leadership that brought us out of that slump and allowed us to win the division. I appreciate Todd and I want to thank him.

I want to thank the people that made this book possible. Joel Kassewitz and his wife, Darcie Glazer Kassewitz. What tremendous people they are. Joel kept asking me, "Why don't you write a book?" And I said, "You find me a co-author and I'll write it."

I truly thank him. I'm so appreciative of them and have so much respect for them and the entire Glazer family. I really want to give a special thanks to Jason Licht, the Bucs' general manager. This will be my sixth season and he does a terrific job. This book would not have been possible without the guidance and encouragement of Keith Wallman, the executive editor and editor in chief of Diversion Books, who was there for us every step of the way. We also would like to thank publisher Scott Waxman and publishing assistant Clara Linoff, whose hard work, counsel, and patience was invaluable to completing this project.

Finally, thanks to Rick Stroud for taking time away from his family to write this book with me.

As I tell people, until you're eighty-five years old, you don't have an idea how great the opportunity is to have a job and go to work. It's the greatest feeling in the world.

I know, eventually, it's going to come to an end. I know, eventually, they're going to have to retire me because I'm never retiring on my own. I want to be very up front about that. I'm never retiring.

Trust me, I have not been cheated. I have lived the greatest life in the world. To quote Lou Gehrig, I consider myself the luckiest man on the face of the earth.

I'm the most fortunate guy in the world to have had an opportunity to have lived the life that I've lived.

I want to thank my family. My wife, Willie, and my children, Terry and Danny. When you live this life of being a coach, collegiately and professionally, a lot of people have to make sacrifices. The sacrifices that my family has made so that I could live a dream are truly appreciated. I can't thank them enough and I hope they know I appreciate them and that I truly love them.

The last thing I want to say is this book was written for one reason: to tell my life story because there's a lot of lessons people can learn from it. In no way have I tried to be critical of anybody and in no way have I tried to second-guess anybody, because I've made a lot of mistakes myself and I've tried to correct them.

I'm an opinionated guy. But as I say, I've tried to correct them. I just hope people can gain things from this book that can help them in their process of developing and advancing in their work or life. If I help one person, if I've given the one piece of advice that helps one coach, this whole book is worth it.

I've been so fortunate. It's a dream come true. People ask, why would you write a book before it all comes to an end? Because I may not be able to write one at that time. I'm hoping they carry me off the football field boots-first because football has been my life.

INDEX

ABOUT THE AUTHORS

TOM MOORE enters his sixth season with the Buccaneers in 2024 and his forty-sixth NFL season overall. The oldest active NFL coach at the age of eighty-five, Moore was honored in 2015 with the Pro Football Writers of America Paul "Dr. Z" Zimmerman Award and later by the Pro Football Hall of Fame with an Award of Excellence for his lifetime contributions as an assistant coach. Following thirteen seasons at the collegiate level and one year in the World Football League, Moore made the jump to the NFL as a wide receivers coach for the Pittsburgh Steelers in 1977. Over his decades in the NFL, his teams have won sixteen diversion titles, played in forty-eight postseason games, and captured four Super Bowl victories. He has coached Hall of Fame players, such as Peyton Manning, Lynn Swann, John Stallworth, Terry Bradshaw, Franco Harris, Mike Webster, Barry Sanders, Marshall Faulk, Randall McDaniel, Cris Carter, Marvin Harrison, and Edgerrin James. Moore has coached alongside four Super Bowl–winning head coaches—Chuck Noll, Mike Ditka, Tony Dungy, and Bruce Arians—all of whom are enshrined in Canton. Moore and his wife, Emily, have two children, daughter Terry and son Dan.

ABOUT THE AUTHORS

RICK STROUD is an award-winning journalist at the *Tampa Bay Times*, having spent three decades covering the Bucs and the NFL. He is a regular contributor to *The Dan Patrick Show*, *The Rich Eisen Show*, NFL Radio, ESPN, and other major national outlets.